Mark Harrell

GENESIS
AND THE
MYSTERY
CONFUCIUS
COULDN'T
SOLVE

D0187693

GENESIS

AND 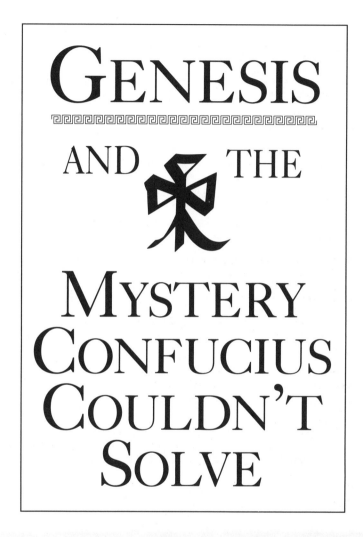 THE

MYSTERY
CONFUCIUS
COULDN'T
SOLVE

Ethel R. Nelson / Richard E. Broadberry

CONCORDIA PUBLISHING HOUSE · SAINT LOUIS

Scripture quotations marked TEV are from the Good News Bible, the Bible in TODAY'S ENGLISH VERSION. Copyright © American Bible Society 1966, 1971, 1976. Used by permission.

Scripture quotations marked KJV are from the King James or Authorized Version of the Bible.

Scripture quotations marked NKJV are from the Holy Bible, New King James Version, copyright © 1979, 1980, 1982 Thomas Nelson, Inc. Used by permission.

Scripture quotations marked RSV are from the Revised Standard Version of the Bible, copyrighted 1946, 1952, © 1971, 1973 by the division of Christian Education of the National Council of the Churches of Christ in the U.S.A., and are used by permission.

Scripture quotations marked NRSV are from the New Revised Standard Version of the Bible, copyright © 1989. Used by permission.

Scripture quotations, unless otherwise indicated, are taken from the HOLY BIBLE, NEW INTERNATIONAL VERSION®. NIV®. Copyright © 1973, 1978, 1984 by International Bible Society. Used by permission of Zondervan Publishing House. All rights reserved.

Originally published as *Mysteries Confucius Couldn't Solve,* © 1986 Ethel R. Nelson. Revised 1994.

Copyright © 1994 Ethel R. Nelson

Published by Concordia Publishing House
3558 S. Jefferson Avenue, St. Louis, MO 63118-3968
Manufactured in the United States of America

All rights reserved. No part of this publication may be reproduced, stored in a retrieval system, or transmitted, in any form or by any means, electronic, mechanical, photocopying, recording, or otherwise, without the prior written permission of Concordia Publishing House.

Library of Congress Cataloging-in-Publication Data

Nelson, Ethel R., 1923–
      Genesis and the mystery Confucius couldn't solve / Ethel R. Nelson
      and Richard E. Broadberry. — Rev. 1994.
      Originally published: Mysteries Confucius couldn't solve. South
      Lancaster, MA:Read Books, 1986.
      ISBN 0-570-04635-1
      1. Chinese language—Etymology. 2. Chinese language—Religious
aspects. 3. Bible. O.T. Genesis—Miscellanea. I. Broadberry, Richard E. II. Title.
PL 1281.N44   1994
299'.5—dc20   93-50090

6 7 8 9 10 11 12 13 14   14 13 12 11 10 09 08 07

To the memory of Pastor Kang Chong Heng, the one who first opened my eyes to the ancient Chinese world and the analysis of its fascinating ideographic characters. What an honor and pleasure it was to work with him in writing a prior book, *The Discovery of Genesis,* fragments of which are used in composing this new work. His influence lives on.

Ethel R. Nelson

To my parents, Mr. and Mrs. N. E. Broadberry; Ron and Doreen Barber; Ray and Yvonne Rona; Stephen Broadberry; and my wife, Maggie; for their love, prayers, and encouragement.

Richard E. Broadberry

Contents

Acknowledgments

From time to time several others have attempted to give biblical analysis to a few of the mysterious Chinese characters. But none, so far as we know, have gone back to the bronzeware and oracle bone inscriptions—the most original, extant forms—as a basis for their interpretation. As you read this book, you will be amazed at the early Chinese people's knowledge of earth's beginnings and how their pictographic and ideographic characters support the veracity of the often-maligned early chapters of the biblical Genesis.

In fact, as Richard Broadberry and I undertook investigation of the oracle bone and bronzeware radicals (the "ABCs") of the writing, we found that about 70 percent were related to the early Chinese people's original knowledge of the Creator God and earth's beginning stories. This convinced us even more that the primitive Chinese, like the ancient Egyptians, produced hieroglyphs illustrating their religious tenets.

With the passage of seven years since the publication of *Mysteries Confucius Couldn't Solve*, it is now time for some revision and enlargement of this work. Seven years ago I stated, "We are not claiming infallibility in our analysis of the characters, for as in any type of research, changes are bound to be made as understanding increases." We found this to be true in several instances. However, we are more convinced than ever, as previously stated, that in the interpretation, "mere coincidence can be ruled out by the hundreds of nicely integrated elements brought together in logical combinations." Furthermore, our conclusion is the same, that "comparison of ancient Chinese and Hebrew concepts of early earth history fits like a tongue-in-groove and helps gel a liquid hypothesis into a solid theory."

In this enlarged edition, we have added approximately 50 new character analyses as well as an appendix in which we have correlated postdiluvian biblical and Chinese history.

We are pleased that Dr. Timothy Boyle has appreciated our study and is using many of these bronzeware and oracle bone character interpretations in a book he has just completed for the Japanese. I want to thank him also for a few analyzed characters he has contributed to this present work.

I especially want to thank my daughter, Laurel Damsteegt, for her patient instruction in Macintosh computer technology, as well as for her invaluable help with PageMaker. She also insisted that I computerize the ancient characters by drawing them with Fontographer on a Wacom tablet. My son Orlyn Nelson, from the Eusey Press in Leominster, Massachusetts, has been my chief printing advisor. I have Jonathon Vance to thank for producing camera-ready copy.

Finally, I will quote once more from the previous edition: "It is hoped that any Chinese philologist who might chance to read this book may not think it too impertinent for two foreigners to invade this ancient precinct and attempt a 'New Look at an Old Language' (see Epilog). We have suggested a number of 'keys' to unlock the greatest mystery of all—that of interpreting what we believe is the true meaning behind many Chinese characters!"

Ethel R. Nelson, M.D.
Dunlap, Tennessee

Artwork on the reverse page by Shunichi Yamamoto.
Copyright © 1993 by Shunichi Yamamoto.
Used by permission.

Altar of Heaven, Beijing, with Temple of Heaven in immediate background

1

The Riddle

*He who understands the ceremonies of the
sacrifices to Heaven and Earth ... would find the
government of a kingdom as easy as to look into
his palm!*
Confucius, *The Doctrine of The Mean*, xix, 6

For 40 centuries the reigning emperors of China had traveled annually to the border of the country or imperial city. There, on an outdoor altar, they sacrificed and burned young unblemished bullocks to *ShangTi* (上帝), the *Heavenly Ruler*. The Border Sacrifice, as it came to be called, was a ceremony conducted in unbroken sequence from the legendary period of Chinese history, before the first dynastic rule which began in 2205 B.C. (see Appendix, p. 143). After a continual observance of more than 4,000 years, this rite ended only in 1911 of our own century. This imperial sacrifice had become closely identified with the rulership of China, for the emperor himself was the chief participant in the ceremony. Consequently, when the Manchus were deposed in 1911, not only the dynastic reign ended forever, but also China's longest celebrated and most colorful sacrifice: the Border Sacrifice.

So important to the mind of the sage Confucius (551-479 B.C.) was this Great Sacrifice that he compared a comprehension of the ritual to the efficient ruling of the Chinese empire. Yet he himself could find no reason for the sacrifice to ShangTi, which remained an unsolved riddle. Why did Confucius attach so much significance to this mysterious Border Sacrifice?

Even the origins of the sacrifices to heaven and earth are enigmatic. One of the earliest accounts is found in the *Shu Ching* (*Book of History*, compiled by Confucius), where it is recorded of Emperor Shun (c. 2230 B.C.) that "he sacrificed to ShangTi."[1] This emphasizes mystery number two: Who is ShangTi?

In the 15th century A.D., the service was moved to the southern part of Beijing, where an extensive park came to quarter three main sacred edifices. In 1420, a great Hall of Prayer for Good Harvests was completed. This northernmost temple is mounted on a triple-tiered, white marble terrace with surrounding balustrades 11 meters (36 feet) high. Fifty thousand blue, glazed tiles (representing the sky) cover a cone-shaped roof, also three-tiered. No nails were used in the construction of the circular wall, which is supported by 28 wooden columns hewn from single trees. In the center are four great pillars, which together with the outer framework support the roof without the use of ceiling joists. The entire interior is painted in multicolor designs.

To the south is a second, smaller Temple of Heaven, the Imperial Vault. Its plan follows the same architecture, except the blue-tiled roof is a single cone. Inside this edifice resides no idol, but a tablet on the north wall is inscribed with the characters 皇天上帝 (*Heavenly Sovereign ShangTi*).

In a straight line, yet farther south, is the altar of sacrifice itself. This great, triple-tiered, white marble Altar of Heaven, 75 meters (250 feet) in diameter, again surrounded on each level by balustrades, has the appearance of a gigantic wedding cake. The uppermost level can be reached by series of steps on each of four sides. A monumental undertaking, construction of it was completed in 1539.

Transport yourself back in time to observe firsthand the events surrounding ancient China's most sacred site and rite. As the winter solstice (about Dec. 22) approaches, the supporting cast readies itself for the glorious ritual. Singers prepare their colorful silken robes; musicians dust off their racks of suspended bronze bells, varying-sized drums, cymbals, flutes, and stringed instruments, dedicated exclusively for use in this annual event.

On the morning before the winter solstice, the emperor, the "Son of Heaven," in gorgeous array passes through the front gate of the Imperial Palace (the Forbidden City) and makes his way in a procession to the Temple of Heaven park. An impressive retinue of princes and high officials follows. The streets of Beijing are silent, as all residents are required to remain hidden behind shuttered windows.

By reviewing the litany of prayers and praises, one may begin to understand the Chinese attitude toward ShangTi. After arriving at the Temple of Heaven, the emperor first meditates in the Imperial Vault, while the costumed singers, accompanied by the musicians, sing the recitation:

> To Thee, O mysteriously–working Maker, I look up in thought. How imperial is the expansive arch (where Thou dwellest).... With the great ceremonies I reverently honour Thee. Thy servant, I am but a reed or willow; my heart is but as that of an ant; yet have I received Thy favouring decree, appointing me to the government of the empire. I deeply cherish a sense of my ignorance and blindness, and am afraid, lest I prove unworthy of Thy great favours. Therefore will I observe all the rules and statutes, striving, insignificant as I am, to discharge my loyal duty. Far distant here, I look up to Thy heavenly palace. Come in Thy precious chariot to the altar. Thy servant, I bow my head to the earth reverently, expecting Thine abundant grace. All my officers are here arranged along with me, joyfully worshipping before Thee.... Oh that Thou wouldest vouchsafe to accept our offerings, and regard us, while thus we worship Thee, whose goodness is inexhaustible![2]

The emperor then makes his way to the Hall of Prayer for Good Harvests.

On the morrow's festive solstice, the emperor returns to the Temple of Heaven Imperial Vault and then proceeds to the Altar of Heaven to perform the sacrificial rituals. The crisp morning air is filled with songs of praise and prayer. (Some of these will be presented at appropriate points in subsequent chapters). Gems and silks are brought forth, as well as vessels of food, and three offerings of wine, all accompanied by music and dances:

> The dances have all been performed, and nine times the music has resounded. Grant, O Te [ShangTi], Thy great blessing to increase the happiness of my house. The instruments of metal and precious stones have

given out their melody. The jeweled girdles of the officers have emitted their tinklings.... While we celebrate His great name, what limit can there be, or what measure? For ever He setteth fast the high heavens, and establisheth the solid earth. His government is everlasting. His unworthy servant, I bow my head, I lay it in the dust, bathed in His grace and glory.[3]

As the sacrificial bullock is burned, a final song resounds:

We have worshipped and written the Great Name on this gem–like sheet. Now we display it before Te, [ShangTi] and place it in the fire. These valuable offerings of silks and fine meats we burn also with these sincere prayers, that they may ascend in volumes of flames up to the distant azure. All the ends of the earth look up to Him. All human beings, all things on the earth, rejoice together in the Great Name.[4]

Today the Temple and Altar of Heaven (T'ien T'an) in Beijing are prime tourist attractions. Few people in the surging crowds that clamber over the worn marble steps even concern themselves with wondering about the origin and meaning of the Great Sacrifice. Centuries ago, the obscure rite that inspired the construction of these cryptic edifices captivated the imagination of Confucius, but even the sage had no answer to the riddle.

Is it possible that we can decipher the puzzle and trace the original intention of this magnificent ceremony of antiquity? We believe so—and by a most unusual means. We will find, strangely enough, that even though the ritual is no longer practiced in China today, it still has great significance for all—for those of the Western world as well as the Orient.

2

Who Is ShangTi?

Chi Lu asked ... "I venture to ask about death?"
The Master answered ... "While you do not know
life, how can you know about death?"
Confucian Analects, Bk. xi, Ch. xi

Do you ever wonder where you came from? Most people do. Some even have a well-kept family record of ancestors, covering many generations. Regardless of whether or not you know who your ancestors were, do you have any idea how humanity and all life on earth came into being or who the very first human beings were?

Some scientists today tell us that humanity has evolved through countless ages from lower forms of life. They say people emerged as upright creatures, descendants of an apelike animal. But did you know that the ancient teachings of the Chinese reveal that the first man and woman on earth were stately, intelligent, specially created beings? They even resembled their great Creator God. This great God, according to the Chinese, made not only people, but the earth and all life in it, as well as the entire universe.

In the earliest Chinese history, this Creator God was called *ShangTi* 上帝 , meaning the *emperor* 帝 *above* 上 . His very name indicates His heavenly rulership. From the most remote time in Chinese history, the sacred Border Sacrifice, described in the previous chapter, was conducted each year for the worship of ShangTi. As the emperor himself took part in this annual service dedicated to ShangTi, the following words, recorded in the collected statutes of the Ming Dynasty (大明會典), were recited, designating ShangTi as the Creator of the world:

> Of old in the beginning, there was the great chaos, without form and dark. The five elements [planets] had not begun to revolve, nor the sun and moon to shine. You, O Spiritual Sovereign [神皇] first divided the grosser parts from the purer. You made heaven. You made earth. You made man. All things with their reproducing power got their being.[1]

ShangTi's continuing regard and love for His created beings are further demonstrated in other recitations from the Border Sacrifice ceremony:

> All the numerous tribes of animated beings are indebted to Thy favour for their beginnings. Men and things are all emparadised in Thy love, O Te. All living things are indebted to Your goodness, but who knows from whom his blessings come to him? You alone, O Lord, are the true parent of all things.[2]

He [ShangTi] sets fast forever the high heaven,

and establishes the solid earth. His government
is everlasting.[3]

Your sovereign goodness cannot be measured. As a
potter, You have made all living things.[4]

From the foregoing we learn that ShangTi made the heavens and the earth and people. He is the true parent of all things. His love is over all His works. His years are without end. His goodness cannot be measured. This is what the ancient Chinese ancestors believed. Could it all be true? Said Confucius in the *Chung-Yung,* "The ceremonies of the celestial and terrestrial sacrifices are those by which men serve ShangTi."[5]

Actually there came to be two border sacrifices. At the summer solstice, a sacrifice to the earth was observed on the northern border; while the offering to Heaven at the winter solstice on the southern border gradually became the more important.

But long before, even before the reign of the Yellow Emperor Huang Ti (黃帝), in the "legendary period" (preceding 2205 B.C.), the Chinese were already offering sacrifices to ShangTi at Mount Tai in Shan-tung, at the *eastern* border of China.[6] A border sacrifice at an eastern locale is most significant, as we shall subsequently learn.

Did ShangTi die along with the imperial reign in China in 1911? The Chinese today certainly are not ignorant of ShangTi, but few really appreciate Him as the original God of China, the creator of heaven and earth. Is it possible that though unknown and unappreciated, ShangTi is still the supreme ruler, not only of the Chinese, but over all of earth's inhabitants, since He created them all?

After the sixth-century B.C. introduction of Confucianism and Taoism, followed by Buddhism from India in the first century B.C., ShangTi was largely forgotten as the one and only God of the Chinese. However, all traces and knowledge of the original God of China have not been erased. We believe a beautiful history of the beginnings of the human race on the newly created planet earth have been perfectly preserved in the ancient character-writing of the Chinese language. The written language was invented simultaneously with the development of the early Chinese culture.

According to tradition, Tsieng Chih, a minister of the same early Yellow Emperor Huang Ti, invented the first characters that have been thought to be simple drawings of familiar objects.[7] Picture words (pictographs) were the earliest form of writing in the ancient world. Other peoples living at the same time in Egypt and Sumeria also had their own pictographic writing. The Chinese inventor of the writing found that, by combining two or more pictographs, a story could be related and, thus, a new idea expressed. In this way, the ideographic (an idea-in-writing) character was born. Of course, in order to be meaningful, ideographs would have to be based upon concepts or knowledge commonly held and understood by these ancient people. Familiar historical events of a sacred nature (such as the creation of the first man and woman, the original relationship between God and people, how sin began and God's remedy for it, etc.) appear to have been the subjects of great interest and were, therefore, incorporated into ideographs—as we shall see.

Once the characters had been invented and accepted, apparently they gradually lost their original historical connections. With the passage of century after century, the origin and true meaning of these characters were lost and became mysterious, even as ShangTi also became mysterious.

To add to the difficulty in analyzing the characters for their true meanings, scribes through the centuries expressed the ideas of the characters with artistic variations, thus producing many ways of writing a single character. Finally, the great conqueror, Ch'in Shih Huang Ti, around 220 B.C., had one of his ministers, Li Ssu, standardize the writing with production of the Lesser Seal script.[8]

There have been minor modifications (such as the Li and Ts'ao) since then, so today's characters are "shorthand" editions of the early pictographs. For this reason, we will examine the most ancient character forms known, especially the bronzeware and oracle bone scripts, to learn the original intention and meanings. On these bronzeware vessel and bone artifacts, the characters are clear pictographs that can be more easily deciphered than today's writing forms.

Bronzeware ceremonial vessels, dating back as far as the Shang dynasty (1711-1122 B.C.), have been beautifully preserved. Many of these contain inscriptions inside the vessels, written, of course, in the character forms of that day. This writing has hence been termed "bronzeware" writing. Characters incised on bones and tortoise shells, used for divination purposes, are another source of the oldest extant Chinese writing. These characters, therefore, are called "oracle bone" writing. Henceforth, in referring to a bronzeware character, the designation will be a subscript $_{(B)}$; for oracle bone characters, the label will be $_{(O)}$; seal characters will be tagged $_{(S)}$ and unidentified ("hybrid," artistic variant) characters as $_{(U)}$. Dictionary definitions of characters are italicized in this book, whereas definitions occasionally interpreted by the authors will be found in quotes or unitalicized.

The first attempt at analyzing the Chinese characters to determine the true meaning of the ancient ideographs was attempted by Hsu Shen in 86 B.C., but his catalog, the *Shuo Wen*, was not published until about A.D. 120. [9] Most Chinese dictionaries are still based upon the *Shuo Wen*. More recent analyses, even in English (e.g., Wieger, Wilder and Ingram), are also largely drawn from the same ancient source.

However, by Hsu Shen's day, Taoist ideas had almost completely replaced the original ancient religious beliefs in a single Creator God, ShangTi. Hsu Shen naturally analyzed the characters according to the current knowledge and thinking of his day. Since the original intentions of the inventor had long since been buried in the dust of passing ages, how could the true ideas behind many of the ancient characters ever be recovered? Or were they to be forever lost—an unsolvable mystery?

The idea of comparing certain Chinese ideographic

characters with another extremely old historical document, the sacred writings of the Hebrew people, has produced startling results. One of the purposes of this book is to bring together and demonstrate the similarity of the historical narratives of the two widely separated Chinese and Hebrew ancient civilizations.

In the epilog, we will comment briefly on the two methods of analysis: the *Shuo Wen* and our "hieroglyphic" system— "hiero" indicating "sacred," and "glyph" meaning "engraving." Were the Chinese pictograms and ideograms drawn from objects and activities of everyday life, or were they more specifically oriented to the ancients' knowledge of sacred history? By the end of the book, you will be better able to judge the merits of the "hieroglyphic" system here introduced.

The oldest of the Hebrew narratives was written about 1500 B.C., at least seven centuries after the Chinese writing came into being. From earliest human memory and tradition, as well as through inspiration from the God of the Hebrews, a prophet, Moses, recorded the beginnings of earth's history. The first book of the Hebrew Scriptures is called Genesis: "Beginnings."

It is indeed interesting to examine the recitation of the Chinese Border Sacrifice rites worshiping ShangTi, with reference to the first verses of the Hebrew Genesis, which also names the Creator God. Read again the recitation given at the beginning of the chapter (p. 20), and note the similarity with excerpts from the more detailed story as recorded in the Hebrew writings:

In the beginning God created the heavens and the earth. The earth was without form, and void; and darkness was on the face of the deep....

Then God said, "Let the waters under the heavens be gathered together into one place, and let the dry land appear"; and it was so. And God called the dry land Earth, and the gathering together of the waters He called Seas....

Then God made two great lights: the greater light to rule the day, and the lesser light to rule the night. He made the stars also....

So God created man in His own image;... male and female He created them. Then God blessed them, and God said to them, "Be fruitful and multiply; fill the earth and subdue it; have dominion over the fish of the sea, over the birds of the air, and over every living thing that moves on the earth."[10]

ShangTi surely appears to be one and the same as the God of the Hebrews. In fact, one of the Hebrew names for God was El Shaddai, phonetically similar to ShangTi, especially in the Cantonese dialect which pronounces the name ShangDai. Cantonese, incidentally, is thought to be closest to the original spoken Chinese.

Let us now begin an investigation of earth's primal history by analyzing some old and simple Chinese characters. At the same time, we will compare stories contained in them with the ancient Hebrew narratives.

3

Chinese Concepts
of Earth's Human Beginnings

The ancient mystery regarding the origin and identity of ShangTi 上帝 has been solved. As we have learned, the Border Sacrifice to ShangTi clearly identifies Him as the Creator God of the universe. The next question is, how did ShangTi create all things? Note one further recitation from this ancient rite:

> When Te [ShangTi], the Lord, had so decreed, He called into existence heaven, earth, and man. Between heaven and earth He separately placed in order men and things, all overspread by the heavens.[1]

Notice that ShangTi, according to the ancient Chinese record, "called into existence heaven, earth, and man." Compare this with the way the Hebrew text describes the method of creation by El Shaddai (who, we suspect, is identical with ShangTi, as the similarity in name and role would suggest):

> The Lord created the heavens by His command, the sun, moon, and stars by His spoken word....When He spoke, the world was created; at His command everything appeared.[2]

The Chinese and Hebrew records are identical. El Shaddai/ ShangTi simply spoke objects into being, as His vast energy, expressed as a command, was transformed into matter, or visible created objects. He thus probably used what has become an elementary law of nature: "Mass and energy can neither be created nor destroyed, but energy can be converted into mass, or mass into energy." Plants and animals sprang into being at His command. But most wonderful of all, His whole creative work of producing not only our earth but also the whole planetary system out of nothing took but six ordinary 24-hour days. The beautiful new earth in perfect order emerged from chaotic darkness.

A summary of the Hebrew Genesis reveals that, on the first day, El Shaddai / ShangTi created light and drove out the darkness that covered the deep rolling waters on the earth's surface. The second day, He divided the waters surrounding the earth and in this space created the atmospheric heavens with their life-supporting gases. The third day, He pushed back the waters over portions of the earth and formed seas. Upon the dry land that appeared, He brought forth vegetation with plants yielding seed to reproduce themselves. At the close of each day He saw that everything was very good.

The fourth day, El Shaddai/ShangTi made the sun, moon, and planets and set them in motion in the heavens to produce the days, months, and seasons. On the fifth day, He brought forth swarms of living creatures in the seas and birds in the skies. All creatures were given reproductive powers.

The sixth day, He said, "Let the earth bring forth the living creature according to its kind … and it was so."[3]

Here, God commanded the earth to bring forth living animals. A bronzeware form of the radical *to produce, bring forth, create* (B)[4] (生) shows God Ψ with arms upraised (we will confirm the symbol Ψ as "God" more conclusively later) and the *earth* (B)[5] (土). Furthermore, the character *to speak, to tell* in the bronzeware form (B)[6] (告) combines *to create* with a *mouth* (O,B)[7] (口). Contained within this one character, we find all the elements of creation: God Ψ creates from the earth by speaking with His mouth 口.

*bring forth
life, beget*

Once again, we'd like to explain our format used throughout the book. It may initially appear rather complicated but actually is quite simple. A subscript in parenthesis following a character indicates the source of the ancient form: (B) = bronzeware; (O) = oracle bone; (S) = seal; (U) = unidentified writing, a hybrid, artistic variation. Use of one of these markers will circumvent having to repeat information regarding the origin of the character in the text. Dictionary definitions of characters are italicized, whereas definitions occasionally assigned by the authors are placed in quotes or unitalicized.

earth

speak, tell

Ψ (Ψ)	+	+	=	+	口	=	
God	dust	bring forth		mouth		to speak, tell	

The foregoing is an illustration for non-Chinese readers, demonstrating how an ideographic character is cleverly formed.

29

The ABCs of Chinese writing are the most primitive symbols, often little pictographs called "radicals." There are 214 of them, e.g., ♦ (土); ⊔ (口). Radicals may be combined to form a more complex radical, as ♦ (生), or with addition of other radical(s), a character, as ♦ (告). In this book, since the ancient forms are more pictographic, they will be used, with today's renditions in parenthesis, e.g., ♦ (告).

It is appropriate, at this point, that more be said concerning the interesting and important radical *mouth* ⊔ (0, B)[7] (口). Just as there are many ancient forms for *mouth*, such as ○ , □ , ▽ , ◇ , so there are also a number of meanings for the radical. The *mouth* has three important functions: speaking, eating, and breathing. Thus, the *mouth* symbols may be used to represent these functions in various characters. The *mouth* may also represent a *person*, even as we may be familiar with the idiom "so many mouths to feed."

mouth, person

We now examine an oracle bone writing for *Ti (ShangTi)* : ♦ (0)[8] (帝). It would appear that ▽ + ▷ + ◁ represent three *persons* in the Godhead (this will be subsequently explained). That a *mouth* ⊔ (口) is used to symbolize ShangTi is significant, as He created by *speaking* things into existence (see recitation, p. 27, and character ♦ , p. 29).

ShangTi, God

The creation of humanity, as well as the land animals, took place on the sixth day but was more special than that of all the other creatures. The actual creation of the first man is pictured in a second name for God, *Shen* ♦ (S)[9] (神). In this character, the left radical ♦ is a "God" radical (this will also be

explained later), but the right radical 〔〕 pictures two *hands* 〔〕
reaching down from above. Hands reaching from above, such
as 〔〕 or 〔 , we will learn, are usually God's hands. (Later,
we will find that hands reaching upward 〔〕 would appear to
be human hands). But what do we find in Shen's hands? The
most primitive drawing of a *person* is │ .

Shen, God

$$ 示 \quad + \quad 〔〕 \quad + \quad │ \quad = \quad 示 $$

God radical   hands   person   God (Shen)

Incidentally, 〔〕 (中) by itself means *to instruct, explain*
and is even more clearly written in a bronzeware inscription
as 〔〕 (B)[10]. Remember that we are looking at very simple

hands

pictures. To make sure we understand that │ is a *person*, a
large dot ● has been added, as 〔 . A large dot ● (B)[11] (丅)
indicates an *adult male*.

$$ 〔〕 \quad + \quad │ \; (中) + \quad ● \quad = \quad 〔〕 $$

hands   person   adult male   to instruct

*instruct,
explain*

The first human being on earth, according to both the Chinese and the Hebrew records, was a fully grown adult man
who came forth from the hands of God (Shen). In the Hebrew
Scriptures, this is the record of man's creation:

> And the Lord God formed man of the dust of the
> ground, and breathed into his nostrils the breath of
> life; and man became a living soul.[12]

We learn that this man's name was "Adam." In the Hebrew,
this means *ground* and also *red.* Note how the Chinese writing

once more agrees with these designations. The radical *soil, earth* (B) (土), as etched inside ancient bronzeware vessels, shows a *person* | , an *adult male* ● , coming up from the ground ___ beneath him.

hole, pit

$$| \quad + \quad ● \quad + \quad \_\_ \quad = \quad \text{(earth symbol)}$$

person   adult male   ground   earth, dust

Several additional characters depict the creation of Adam from the dust of the earth.

noble man

The Chinese character for *hole, pit* (S)[13] (臽) pictures God's *hands* (臼) scooping *man* (人) from a *hole* in the ground. The radical (O)[14] (立) is a pictogram of a *noble man* standing on the ground ___ . This radical has a number of significant meanings: *to stand, establish, found, create, start,* all of which, in displaying Adam coming up out of the ground, represent the original *creation* of humanity, the founding, establishing, starting of the human race. A further meaning of is *immediately, at once.* This would suggest that Adam's creation was instantaneous, that the process was not a slowly evolving formation. This concept is

stand, create, establish, start

borne out by an additional character indicating *a moment, an instant* (S)[15](叟), where the *man* (人) is being released from the Creator God's *hands* (手).

a moment, an instant

Yet another character depicting the first man arising from the dust of the earth is (B) (O)[16] (壬), indicating *great.* Note that the *man* arises from the *earth, soil* (土). The oracle bone symbol for *earth* may be written as ,

great

△ , ⊥ , or ♀. Each indicates a *person* ◇ , △ , | , or ○ , arising from the ground ___ beneath.

earth, soil

Another representation of the creation of Adam is found in the radical, *body* 𝌰 (B)[17] (身). This radical is phonetically similar to Shen (God). Adam's was the first human body formed on the new earth. ⌐ (B)[18] (人) represents a *person* or *being*, in this instance, the Creator who is bending over an object. He may be more clearly perceived if we draw a head on the pictogram: (⌐). Adam is this time depicted as ⊙ , and note he is being formed from the earth beneath ___ . If you are acquainted with ancient Chinese, you might be thinking ⊙ (B)[19] (日) means *sun*. But ⊙ also means *person*. Therefore, the character *dawn, early morning* ♀ (S)[20] (旦), has a clever double meaning. Adam must have been created from the ground ___ at *dawn* ♀ on the sixth day.

body

Why should Adam be represented as a *sun* ⊙ ? Actually, we see a pictogram of a *person, mouth* ○ (B) (口). Recall again the common idiom in designating *persons:* so many *mouths* to feed. The small dot · in the center represents *a flame of fire.*

⊙

sun, person

	+	·	=	⊙	+	___	=	♀
person		flame of fire		sun, person		ground		dawn

♀

dawn

Adam had a fiery appearance, as the brightness of the sun, for we learn from the Hebrew Genesis:

> Then God said, "And now We will make human beings; they will be like Us and resemble Us."[21]

33

How is ShangTi (Shen) often perceived? The Hebrew Scriptures again inform us: "The Lord God is a sun and shield."[22] They also say that our "God is a consuming fire."[23] A bronzeware inscription for *fire* is (B)[24](火). This would also support the idea that the first *adult male* • , who was formed from the *dust* of the earth, had the appearance of *fire* , as well as the *sun* ⊙ .

fire

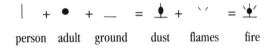

	+ •	+ ___	=	+ ` ´	=
person	adult	ground	dust	flames	fire

To be created resembling God meant Adam was perfect and sinless, even as ShangTi (Shen) is perfect. ShangTi's dazzling perfection is spoken of as His "glory," which is represented as a fiery or sun-like appearance. Therefore was Adam, the first man, originally clothed in a glorious, shining light, even as God? Again, we read from the Hebrew sacred writings:

> O Lord my God, You are very great: You are clothed with honor and majesty, Who cover Yourself with light as with a garment.[25]

The character *to be like* (B)[26] (若) must surely refer to the very fact of Adam's likeness to God. In we recognize not one God, Ψ with arms upraised, but three acting together as one! How can this be? Review again the Hebrew text:

to be like

> Then God [Elohim] said: "And now We will make human beings; they will be like Us and resemble Us."[27]

Here, the name used for "God" is Elohim, a plural noun. Note also the plural pronouns "We" and "Us." As we proceed, we will find both the Chinese and the Hebrews had the same concept of God—three divine persons working as one, called the Trinity. We will shortly find other examples of this.

Cheng Hsuan, a scholar of the early Han dynasty, stated: "T'ien (Heaven) is another name for ShangTi. "[28] So the Chinese have a third name (besides ShangTi 帝 and Shen 示申 for God: *T'ien, Heaven* 大 (B)[29] 大 (S)[30] (天). As we have studied the bronzeware characters, it appears that a "blackening" of a symbol indicates "glory." We find this in the character for *Heaven* 大 , where the "head" is blackened. (Note the seal character 大 has the *sun* ☉ for a head.) By itself, 大 (B)[31] (大) represents a *great, noble, eldest, adult* person, Adam, made in the image of God, *T'ien, Heaven* 大 . This "blackening," representing God's glory, would also explain why God's fingers are "blackened" in ⊂ Ʒ (p. 31). Note also the depiction of God's *hand(s)* ᐳ , ⋐ , ⊂ Ʒ , always showing just three "fingers," symbolizing the Trinity at work.

T'ien, Heaven

We can understand, too, why Adam, the first *adult male* ● , created in the image of God, *Heaven* 大 (天), was also portrayed as a "glorious" person.

noble man, great, adult

In summary, before Adam sinned and disobeyed God, the Chinese characters portray his body as being covered with a glorious light, as having a fiery appearance. The Hebrew text comments:

> The man and his wife were both naked,
> and they felt no shame.[32]

Adam, and later his wife, were unashamed to appear naked

naked, red

fire

*intelligent,
civilized*

father

before ShangTi. Why? The Chinese character *naked, red* 金 (B)[33] (赤) shows a *noble man* 大 (大) and a *fire* 业. Adam and his wife were made in the image of God, pictured as a covering glorious fire (possibly also red-tinged). Since the Hebrew name "Adam" means not only "ground," but also "red," it may have been this imagery of a fiery covering that made both the Chinese and the Hebrews describe him as being red.

> You have made them [people] a little lower than God, and crowned them with glory and honor.[34]

$$大 (大) \quad + \quad 业 \quad = \quad 金$$

noble man   fire   naked, red

This same fiery appearance is also seen in the significant character *intelligent, civilized* 文 (B)[35] (文), which confirms and records Adam's *refinement*. Earth's first man, 文 , is here decorated with a glorious *flame* · , indicating again his likeness to God.

Analysis of ancient Chinese characters reveals that our world's first man had been formed perfect, sinless, and noble in body and character. His origin was from ShangTi Himself and not from a spontaneous evolutionary process which would eliminate ShangTi as Creator.

We examine yet another Chinese character representing God. The original bronzeware pictograph for *father* (B)[36] (父) likely refers to God, the heavenly parent. Note the "blackening" (glory) of this "ethereal appearing" person with uplifted arms, characteristic of God. Review once more the Border Sacrifice recitation:

> All the numerous tribes of animated beings are indebted to Thy favour for their beginning. Men and things are all emparadised in Thy love, O Te. All living things are indebted to your goodness, but who knows from whom his blessings come to him. You alone, O Lord, are the true parent of all things.[37]

Frequently encountered on the bronzeware is this association, ⚬⅄ (B),[38] once more suggesting the heavenly *Father* ⅄ "forming" Adam, the first *adult male* • .

We promised earlier to identify the symbol Ψ as God (⅄ , p. 29; ⅋, p. 34). To do so, we first examine a new character 畐 (B)[39] 畐 (O)[40] (甫), meaning *father, beginning,* and *garden*. These three meanings find relevance only in reference to creation. The *Father* (God), in the *beginning*, created a beautiful *Garden* of Eden.

garden, father, beginning

$$\Psi\ (\ \varphi\ )\ +\ \boxplus\ =\ \text{畐}\ ,\ \text{畐}$$

Father	garden	garden, Father, beginning

A "shorthand" writing of *Father* ⅄ (God) is therefore written as Ψ .

A specific detail of Adam's creation is found in the character *vessel* ⚬ (B)[41] (自). This time, the *Being* ○ (God) is enfolding the "*dust*man," ⚊ (B) (土), Adam. But why is Adam called a *vessel*? Recall that in the Border Sacrifice recitation, ShangTi was referred to as a potter :

vessel

Your sovereign goodness cannot be measured. As a
potter You have made all living things.[42]

Compare this Chinese concept with the Hebrew Scripture:

Yet, O Lord, You are our Father. We are the clay, You
are the potter; we are all the work of Your hand.[43]

How fitting that Adam should be called a vessel, for he had
been sculpted from clay, the dust of the ground. But more than
this fashioning by the Potter was involved in Adam's creation.

And the Lord God formed man of the dust
of the ground, and breathed into his nostrils the
breath of life; and man became a living soul.[44]

breath

God's second act was to breathe life into Adam, whom He
had formed from the dust of the ground. There are several
radicals and characters for *breath*. The most simple is
$\equiv$ (O)[45] $\odot\!\!\equiv$ (S)[46] (气). Might the three strokes $\equiv$ represent again the Trinity working together in creation (see Elohim,
p. 34)? In $\odot\!\!\equiv$, we find the *breath* $\equiv$ entering and animating
the glorious *person* $\odot$, Adam.

But let us examine another *breath* 气 (O)[47](風). You will
recall that ㅂ (口) represents not only a *mouth,* but also a
person. (The *mouth* also functions in breathing). In 气 , we
find a large inverted *mouth* ∩ (God's) over a smaller, horizontal *mouth* ⊏ (Adam's). Into Adam's mouth, we find the
breath $\equiv$ of life entering.

breath

A similar character, 合 (O)[48] 合 (B)[49] (命), means *to
cause, to order, to summon, excellent.* This time the *mouth*
is written as $\triangledown$, another variation of ㅂ . God's *mouth*

△ covers the smaller, reclining *person* ▷ into which the breath ᴌ is entering, bringing Adam to his knees. The second bronzeware figure depicts Adam, made in God's glorious image ⵁ, resembling *T'ien, Heaven* 夨. God *imprinted* 钞 (B)[50] (印) His own character upon the man ⴷ, Adam, when He created him by His *hand* ⸱.

to summon, cause, order, excellent

We concluded previously that Adam had been formed at dawn on the sixth day of earth's first week (p. 33). All during that day he was given the intriguing task of naming the animals as the great Potter formed them.

> So He [God] took some soil from the ground and formed all the animals and all the birds. Then He brought them to the man to see what he would name them; and that is how they all got their names. So the man named all the birds and all the animals; but not one of them was a suitable companion to help him.[51]

imprint

It was not ShangTi's intention to leave Adam without a mate. So as this first momentous sixth day was drawing to a close, we read again from the Hebrew writings:

> Then the Lord God said, "It is not good for the man to live alone."[52]

What God implied was that it was *good* 好 (B)[53] (好) for Adam, His *son*, 孑 (0)[54] (子) to have a *woman* 宀 (B)[55] (女) for a mate.

good

woman	+	son	=	good

son

If a second *person* ⊔ (口) is added to the previous

woman

character *to call, summon* 兆 (合), we find another significant symbol: *life, will of God, mandate of heaven* 合卩 (B)[56] (命).

> The spirit of God has made me,
> and the breath of the Almighty
> gives me life.[57]

will of God, life

It would be from this first man and woman that all human life would be derived.

Was Adam's mate to be made of the soil as he had been? No, this was not God's beautiful and meaningful purpose. Adam would appreciate his wife even more when he learned ShangTi's unique plan for the creation of woman!

40

4

The Rib Story

As the sixth glorious day of creation was drawing to a close and the sun was beginning to sink toward the western horizon, Adam expressed his wonder that God had not provided a companion for him. Each of the animals, which he had just spent the day naming, had a mate by its side.

vessel

Recall the character ⍢ (B) (卣), *vessel,* illustrating Adam's creation (p. 37). Another ancient artistic depiction of this symbol is ⍥ (B)[1] showing the glorious *flame of fire* · (p. 33). Let us now examine a similar "flasklike" figure: the radical *west* ⍰ (B)[2] (西), which portrays God, a *Being* ◌ , this time enclosing *two* ꞊ *persons* ｜ .

west

◌ (◌)	+	꞊	+	｜ (͏)	=	⍰
God (a Being)		two		person(s)		west

It was evidently as the sun was setting in the west that God brought forth the second person. The details of God's plan are most interesting. We learn from the Hebrew record that God said,

"I will make a suitable companion to help him."...

Then the Lord God made the man fall into a deep sleep, and while he was sleeping, he took out one of the man's ribs and closed up the flesh. He formed a woman out of the rib and brought her to him.[3]

to marry, dusk

A second character which confirms the time and method of creating Adam's mate is 𝄞 (O)[4] (昏), meaning both *dusk* and *to marry*. In 𝄞 we find the great *Being* (God) 𝄫 bending over the *glorified person* ⊙ (日), Adam. Having these two widely divergent meanings—*dusk* and *to marry*—it can only be interpreted as God (𝄫) performing the first operation in which He removes a rib from the sleeping Adam (⊙ , p. 33), and from it forms a beautiful wife for him. Again, it emphasizes the time of day, *dusk*, when Adam's mate was created and the first *marriage* performed by God Himself.

dusk, evening

To further confirm that it was at dusk when Eve was created, let's look at a second character meaning *evening, dusk :* 𝄞 (O)[5] (晏). In this we find God's hands 𝄫 "operating" on the sunlike Adam ⊙ , from whom a *woman* 𝄫 (O)[6] (女) emerges.

woman

We can even see this very operation in today's radical form *flesh* 肉 , where 冂 is *entered* 入 to take out a *person* 人 . But it is even more clear in the ancient form from which today's radical was possibly transcribed: 𝄞 (U)[7] (肉). Here, 𝄫 (人) represents a *man*, Adam, while we find 𝄫 (O)[8] (子) attached to him, meaning not only a *son, offspring*, but also a *bride* or *wife*! Note God's *hand* 𝄫 (B)[9] (𠂇)

reaching inside the *man* ∩ to bring out the *wife* ℐ. And what did Adam exclaim upon awakening?

> "At last, here is one of my own kind—bone taken from my bone, and flesh from my flesh. 'Woman' is her name because she was taken out of man." [10]

flesh

∩ (∩) + ⩕ + ℐ = ᚖ

person   hand (God's)   wife   flesh

A second way of writing the radical for *flesh*, ꓓ (O)[11] (肉), must also be derived from the time of Eve's creation, for *moon* ꓓ (B)[12] ꓓ (O)[13](月) and *evening* ꓓ , ꓓ (B)[14] (夕) are similar pictograms.

bride, wife, son, offspring

Surely, the ancient Chinese as well as the Hebrews knew as fact the earliest history of the world and the creation of man and woman!

Since man was created to resemble God, we would expect that he be similar in appearance. Hence the Chinese pictogram for *man* ∩ (as in ᚖ) resembles the depiction of God as a *being* ⌐ (as in ᚖ and ⊙). This similarity should be borne in mind as we proceed to analyze characters.

moon

What joy Adam knew, especially when he realized that Eve, as he now named his companion, was actually a part of him! God also must have *enjoyed* ⊙ (B)[15] (享) seeing the first pair so happy with each other. A *vessel* ⊙ (B) (㒼) is an apt description of Adam, formed from clay by the heavenly Potter. From the *vessel*, we find a second *person* ○ (口) emerging—depicting the origin of Eve from Adam.

evening

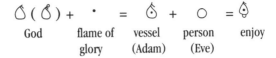

	God	flame of glory	vessel (Adam)	person (Eve)	enjoy

enjoy

In Adam's expression of joy,

"This is now bone of my bones
And flesh of my flesh;
She shall be called Woman,
Because she was taken out of Man," [16]

we can see his *satisfaction* (o)[17] (妾) with the *woman* 女 that God's *hand* had *prepared* for him.

God's hand	+	woman	=	satisfactory, prepare

satisfactory, prepare

God knew that just two persons were *sufficient* (B)[18] (壽) to populate the earth, for He announced to them,

"Be fruitful and multiply, and fill the earth and subdue it; and have dominion ... over every living thing that moves upon the earth." [19]

sufficient

In , we find the Trinity again, the three persons of the Godhead, who took part in creation. (See , p. 34 , with uplifted arms: . Compare this character also with the preceding one, .)

So close was the relationship between the Creator and the first couple that we find them an integral part of *Shen's* (s)[20] (神) name in many different ways of writing it. In this rendition, we find Adam and Eve once more portrayed as *suns, glorified persons* , while God is the great *Being* leaning over them.

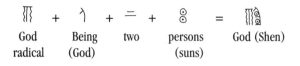

| God radical | + | Being (God) | + | two | + | persons (suns) | = | God (Shen) |

In yet another artistic variation of *Shen* 祁৪ (U)[21] (神), we see the couple conjoined. This appears to be a modification of a bronzeware depiction, *to instruct* ᴀᵤ (B)[22] (申). The very fact that there are not two *suns* in the heavens supports our interpretation that these *suns, persons* ৪ represent the glorified, sinless Adam and Eve. Furthermore, the inscription ᴀᵤ depicts two *mouths, persons* ⊔ (口).

Shen (God)

The bond between God and the first couple is portrayed also in *filial, to honor one's parent* 𝕩 (B)[23] (孝). God is found with upraised arms 𝕩 , and the clever ancient Chinese melded this symbol with the *Father* (God) 乂 (父), while 𝒚 (子) is a *person, offspring* (Adam).

instruct

| 𝕩 | + | 乂 | + | 𝒚 | = | 𝕩 |
| *God'* | | *Father* | | *offspring* | | *filial* |

Another rendition of *filial* 𝕩 (B)[24] varies slightly but carries exactly the same meaning. God, this time, is replaced by ≡ , three strokes that are seen repeatedly in Chinese script. We believe the symbol ≡ represents "God's presence," the Trinity, the three persons of the Godhead. In the pictogram 𝕩 , we find there are *two* ˇ *offspring* 𝒚 , both Adam and Eve.

filial, honor one's parents

| ≡ | + | 乂 | + | ˇ | + | 𝒚 | = | 𝕩 |
| God's presence | | Father | | two | | offspring | | filial |

We are thus given the idea of God as a parent and 𑀘 as two *offspring*. We may now also understand why in *flesh* 𑀘 , the *wife* 𑀘 , Eve, was as an "offspring" of Adam, formed from his very body!

What was the home that God prepared for Adam and Eve like? According to the ancient Chinese, it was a *palace* 𑀘 (B)[25], 𑀘 (O)[26] (宮). Under the *roof* ⌂ are two *persons* ▽ + ▽ (or □ + □) cleverly united as 𑀘 and 𑀘. ShangTi conducted the first marriage ceremony, as the Hebrew text describes it:

palace

> For this reason a man ... [is] united to his wife, and they will become one flesh.[27]

An alternate pictogram of *palace* 𑀘 (U)[28] shows this exactly, where under one *roof* ⌢ (宀), the *couple* 𑀘 (呂) are united as one *flesh* 𑀘 (肉).

couple

𑀘	+	𑀘	+	⌢	=	𑀘
couple		flesh		roof		palace

The character *to unite, join* 𑀘 (O)[29] (立立) pictures the first couple, hand in hand, joined in marriage.

One additional text from the Hebrew script should be quoted at this point:

join, unite

> The man and the woman were both naked, but they were not embarrassed.[30]

There was a reason why they were not embarrassed. They had been made in God's image (see *naked*, p. 36). An additional common character, meaning both *light* and *bare, naked,* 🜚 (O)31 🜚 (O)32 (光), also pictures both the *man* 🜚 and the *woman* 🜚 , although *naked,* covered with *fire* 🜚 , 🜚 .

light, bare,
naked

🜚 (🜚) + 🜚 (🜚) = 🜚 (🜚)
man (woman)　　　fire　　　　naked, light

fire

ShangTi *completed* ☥ (B)33 (十) creating the earth in but six 24-hour days. This radical, *complete, perfect* ☥ , clearly shows the finishing of God's work. The last creative act was to *bring forth* ⸸ human beings. The first *person* | , an *adult male* • , was created from the *dust of the ground* ⊥ . He was *perfect* ☥ and holy. Eve, in turn, was formed from Adam later on this sixth day. The creation of these first two humans *completed* ☥ the earth and its furnishings. We read from the Hebrew writings:

*perfect,
complete*

> Thus the heavens and the earth were completed in all their vast array. By the seventh day God had finished the work He had been doing; so on the seventh day He rested from all His work. And God blessed the seventh day and made it holy, because on it He rested from all the work of creating that He had done.[34]

One can see that the ancient Chinese, as well as the Hebrews, understood that the seventh day was blessed, for the older symbol 十 (B)35 (七), *seven,* shows the familiar pose of God with arms outstretched (🜚). Another rendition for *seven,* 🜚 (S)36 (七), portrays God even more unmistakably, sitting with arm upraised in blessing (🜚).

seven

47

home

The first couple's *home* ⌂ (O)[37] (宅) was established as the seventh 七 day was ushered in. The house ⌂ is depicted, as well as *seven* 七 .

The word *to rest, stop* 𐌅 (B)[38] 𐌏 (O)[39] (止) likewise has significance in the original writing. This radical is used in many characters, as we shall soon discover. These radicals, 𐌅 and 𐌏 , are simple pictographs of a foot. From the "blackening" of 𐌅 , we can gather that it represents ShangTi's foot, *stopped* or *resting* from His six days' work of creating the earth and its contents. Note that the character *blessing* 示𐌏 (O)[40] (祉), for example, contains the God radical 示 (p. 31) and *to rest, stop* 𐌏 (止), making it clear that 𐌏 is God's foot. (The God radical in oracle bone writing is simply 示 (O)[41] (示), indicating a *person* 丨 from *heaven* —).

rest, stop

blessing

God radical

Thus the weekly cycle of seven days was established at creation and has been kept ever since, worldwide, as *the returning seventh day* 七日來復 (a Chinese saying). The week is not regulated by the movement of the earth, sun, moon, or stars but reflects only the great historic work of the Creator, ShangTi. He gave this day of rest to Adam and Eve and their descendants, so that people everywhere might weekly remember His great creative acts.

Secrets of a Lost Garden

From the Chinese writing, we learn that in the *beginning* 夽 (B)[1] (元), there were just *two* 二*persons* 亻 on earth. Furthermore, another bronzeware rendition of *beginning* 夽 (B)[2] reveals that the original couple had sinless characters. They were reflectors of *God, heaven* 大 (天).

beginning

$$二 \ + \ 亻 (亻) + \ \bullet \ = \ 夽$$

   two   persons   "glorious"   beginning
                           (Godlike)

The man was named Adam, meaning "the ground," from which he had been created by God. We learned that the Chinese radicals for *ground, earth* 坴 (B), 𠙵 , 亼 , 丄 (o) (土) all have reference to Adam (review p. 36). And we learned that "Adam called his wife's name Eve, because she was the mother of all living."[3]

Thus we find a record of the first two *ancestors* 𠅘 , 𠃊 (o)[4] (祖). Comparing 亼 and 𠙵 above, representing

ancestor, founder, prototype, original

Adam arising from the earth, we find not only Adam, but *two* persons, he and his wife, Eve, "the mother of all living." The *ancestors* ᵀ⊟ are found with the God radical ⊤ , indicating that ShangTi is, of course, the ultimate ancestor in whose image Adam and Eve had been created. This character denotes not only *ancestor,* but also the *founder, prototype, original, beginning.*

connecting link

$$\top \ + \ = \ + \ \bigcirc \ + \ - \ = \ ^{\top}⊟$$

God radical	two	persons (mouths)	ground	ancestor, prototype

Furthermore, the Chinese make clear that the ultimate Ancestor, or *connecting link* ⟨ (0)[5] (系), is God. In this character, ⟨ represents God (see p. 29), while ⟨ symbolizes the first couple. A second oracle bone form of this symbol makes certain that God is intended as the ultimate *connecting link*, with His *hand* ⟨ pictured. The multiplied *persons* ⟨⟨ would appear to indicate this truth holds for future generations as well.

Just what kind of an environment did ShangTi provide for our first parents? From the Hebrew Scripture, we read a description.

> And the Lord God planted a garden in Eden, in the east; and there He put the man whom He had formed. And out of the ground the Lord God made to grow every tree that is pleasant to the sight and good for food, the tree of life also in the midst of the garden, and the tree of the knowledge of good and evil.

garden,
landed
property

> A river flowed out of Eden to water the garden, and
> there it divided and became four rivers.[6]

This garden paradise has actually been illustrated with drawings in the Chinese calligraphy. A much-used radical *garden,
landed property* ⊞ (B)[7] (田) would seem to have reference
specifically to this first lovely Garden of Eden. At first glance, it
appears to be a well-irrigated field, but the bronzeware inscription, depicted as ⊞ , presents a different idea, especially in light of the Hebrew description that there was a river,
which divided into four rivers, flowing out of Eden to water the
garden. According to this pictograph, the river originated in
the very center, with streams flowing in four directions ✛ .

A second ancient form, 𝄞 (U)[8] (田), gives additional
insight, revealing the wellspring of the four-headed river, as we
shall discover in the next paragraph.

fountain

We immediately wonder what the source of the river might
be. Most rivers originate from converging streams high in the
mountains. Let us examine an earlier form of *spring, fountain* 𝄞 (B)[9] (泉), which portrays a fountain gushing upward and bears resemblance to the aforementioned 𝄞 figure
of *garden*. But note ⊤ (O)[10](示) inscribed on it—an ancient symbol for God!

God radical

A character phonetically similar to *beginning* 元 *(yüan)*
portrays our first parents and is a second pictograph of their
Eden home, *garden* 𝄞 (S)[11] (園), also *yüan*. The closeness
in sound of these pairs of characters seems more than mere
coincidence.

garden

Let us examine this most commonly used character for *garden* 園. We find God Ψ with upraised arms (compare ⚲ p. 29; ⚲ p. 34; ⚲ p. 37; ⚲ p. 44; ⚲ p. 45). By now, it has become more convincing that this figure Ψ represents God. Here He is found on the summit of a *mountain* ∧. Below is a *mouth* □, representing communion: speaking and eating with God. Beneath these are two *persons* ∧∧, the second emerging from the side of the first, even as Eve was created from Adam's rib (pp.42, 44). The garden is *enclosed* □ by a boundary.

Ψ + ∧ + □ + ∧∧ + □ = 園

God · mountain · mouth · persons · enclosure · garden

Listen to what the Hebrew text tells us about God's mountain, the river, the fountain, and the people:

> Thy righteousness is like the mountains of God,...
> How precious is Thy steadfast love, O God!
> The children of men take refuge in the shadow of
>   Thy wings.
> They feast on the abundance of Thy house,
> and Thou givest them drink from the river of Thy
>   delights.
> For with Thee is the fountain of life.[12]

Again, both the Chinese characters and the Hebrew Scripture portray several identical features of the first garden home:

1. A four-headed river flows from the *garden* ⊞ and waters it.

2. The source of the river is a *fountain* 泉 in the center.

3. The *fountain* 𝕽 is symbolic of *God* ⊤ as the "fountain of life."

4. The *garden* 🖾 encompasses God's *mountain* ⌃ , His "house" or dwelling place.

5. Two *persons* ⋏⋏ , "the children of men," come to commune there with God. (This includes feasting—apparently on fruit from the tree of life—and drinking from the river of life. Eating and drinking from these two sources assured Adam and Eve of immortality.)

male, baron

The ancient Chinese give us several picture-words of the first couple in their garden home. First, we'll analyze the character *male, baron* ⊞ (0)[13] (男). The *garden* ⊞ is recognized. The second radical, *power, strength* ⟋ (0)[14] (力), needs some amplification. ⟋ is a pictogram of an arm, in fact, of God's *right* arm. Note this text from the Hebrew Scripture:

power, strength

> With My great power and outstretched arm
> I made the earth and its people and the animals that
> are on it, and I give it to anyone I please.[15]

landlord

Apparently, God is giving the Garden of Eden to Adam, the first male, a "baron." But just what is a baron? A dictionary definition is "a tenant holding his rights and title directly from the king—a nobleman."[16] Adam, the *noble man* 大 , received his land, the Garden of Eden, from the king, God. Furthermore, both Adam and Eve became *landlords* ⊞ (0)[17] (畯), as this pictogram shows. We recognize the *garden* ⊞ and Adam ᘝ (see p. 39), while ᕕ (0)[18] (厶) indicates a

certain person, secret

certain person, Eve. Note that they are again joined, in this figure 틀 .

The *garden* 田 became their *imperial domain* 甸 (O) [19] (甸). You will recognize the *person* ㇏ (Adam). The Hebrew Scriptures record:

cultivate

> Then the Lord God took the man and put him in the garden of Eden to tend and keep it.[20]

Yet another character is relevant: *to cultivate* 畋 (O) [21] (畋). This time we find it is the *Father* (God) 父 (父) who has given the first couple a work to do in the garden.

trees

Recall that two specific trees, the tree of life and the tree of the knowledge of good and evil, were mentioned previously in the Eden description.

> In the middle of the garden were the tree of life and the tree of the knowledge of good and evil.[22]

These two important *trees* 林(O, B) [23] (林), therefore, must have been located on the mountain in the center of the garden. We have already specified that the fountain was symbolic of God and was the source of the four-headed river of life that originated from the center of the garden. The radical meaning *center, place*, 方 (O) [24] (方), provides most interesting

center, place

information. In 方 , we find a *Person* ㇒ containing three symbols for *God* ㇐ , ㅜ , ㄱ , the Trinity (compare *ShangTi* 帝 , p. 30. The bronzeware inscription for this radical, on the other hand, usually shows God with arms outstretched 大 (B) [25] (方). Compare again the bronzeware rendering of *Father* 𑒐 (父). We can thus surmise how ㅜ became an early symbol for God.

It was to this central place in the garden that Adam and Eve *traveled* 𐤎 (B)[26] (旅). The clever ancient Chinese calligrapher simply stretched out the radical *central* 大 and formed God on the holy mountain 𐤇 . The two *persons* 𐤏 are easily recognized.

travel

$$\Psi \quad + \quad \cap \quad = \quad ㅜ \quad + \quad 𐤏 \quad = \quad 𐤎$$

God   mountain   central   two persons   to travel

Another character also meaning *to travel*, 𐤎 (B)[27] (柷), agrees with our interpretation that a *sun* ⊙ (日) frequently depicts a glorified *person* ○ (口), in this case, a human *couple* 𐤑 (呂 , pp. 44-45). Here the *couple* 𐤑 is found at the *tree* 木 of life to which they *traveled* 𐤎 to partake of the fruit giving immortality.

travel

A similar character, 𐤒 (B)[28] (柬), *to invite, pick*, must likewise depict the *tree* 木 of life. The holy couple ⊕ (two sunlike *persons* conjoined) had been *invited* to pick fruit from the tree of life. They *returned* 𐤓 (O)[29] (旋) there frequently. Again, their destination was the holy mount 𐤇 . They *rested* 𐤔 (止) and communed (spoke and ate with God), as specified by the *mouth* ○ (口).

invite, pick

return

$$\Psi \quad + \quad \cap \quad = \quad ㅜ \quad + \quad 𐤔 + \quad ○ \quad = \quad 𐤓$$

God   mount   central   rest   mouth   to return

A second character for *stop, rest*, 𐤕 (B)30 (休), reveals a *person* 𐤖 (Adam or Eve) at the *tree* 木 . As the Hebrew

place

text stated, the two special trees were in the middle of the garden and therefore must have been located on the holy mountain. We can identify this mountain as a holy *place* 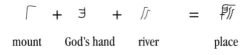 (B)[31] (所), for we find God's *hand* ⸢ (see pp. 31-32) there. Note the mount ⸢ from which the *river* ⼃ of life flows.

$$⸢ \quad + \quad ⼃ \quad + \quad ⼃ \quad = \quad 所$$

mount   God's hand   river   place

hill

We can erase the last doubt that the Garden of Eden had a holy *hill* (O)[32] (B)[33] (陵) when we examine this character. The *mount*, (B) (阝) is identified by three *mouths* (the Trinity) or "God's presence" ☰ . In , we find the *couple*, while in , only Adam as the "*dust*man" appears before *God* ✕ , the *Father* .

mount

$$☰ + | = ⻖ \quad + \quad ⼀ \quad + \quad ✕ \quad + \quad ⼂ \quad = 陵$$

God's   (incline)   mount   "dustman"   God   Father   hill
presence

Let us make one more relevant comparison with the Hebrew record, which reads:

> Who shall ascend the hill of the Lord?
>   And who shall stand in His holy place?
> He who has clean hands and a pure heart,
>   who does not lift up his soul to what is false,
>   and does not swear deceitfully.
> He will receive blessing from the Lord.[34]

It surely seems that the Hebrew Scripture and the Chinese ideographs are describing the same place and activity. Adam and Eve could *travel* 🝖 to the *hill* 🝖 of the Lord and stand in His holy *place* 🝖 , the mountain. They could come before *God* ⊤ and receive *blessing* ⊤℧ from Him.

Why did the early Chinese repeat the theme of the first human couple coming to worship God on the holy mountain in so many meaningful characters? They were able to *visit* 𝒟 , 𝒟 (B)[35] (省) eye to eye ⊘ with their Creator God Ψ , the one who had *created* ⍟ all things everywhere on earth. This face-to-face communion with God was a rare privilege; this *consulting together, visiting* 🜏 (B)[36] (參) would not always be theirs to enjoy. Adam, the first *man* ⌐ , would not always be able to *consult* 🜏 with the members of the "Godhead" 🜏 in this manner. (Note the three, joined *mouths* 🜐 and "God's presence" ⫽). We will learn the reason for his estrangement from God as we continue our study.

visit

eye

*consult
together,
visit*

6

More on the Nature of ShangTi

How delighted Adam and Eve must have been with their beautiful surroundings in the Garden of Eden! Their loving Creator Father, ShangTi, had provided everything for their comfort and benefit. On every hand were luscious fruit-bearing trees and gorgeous flowers of many colors. In the very center of the garden, four sparkling rivers streamed from the sides of a magnificent mountain, God's earthly dwelling place.

mountain

Eden's special mountain, which was visited by ShangTi, becomes more intriguing as we consider additional characters related to it. In the Hebrew Scripture, God's place of *rest* (B) (止), or dwelling place, is called the "hill of the Lord" or "His holy place."

fire

Consider some additional ancient forms of mountain: (B)[1], (O)[2], (B)[3], (O)[4] (山). These are especially significant because of their similarity to the radicals for *fire* on the oracle bones: (O)[5], (O)[6], (O)[7] (火).

From this we can assume that God's glorious, holy presence, as a fire, enshrouded His holy mountain.

burning

For example, examine the character meaning *burning*: 燓 (O)[8] (燓). We find here a *mountain* ○, but the symbol ○ also indicates *fire*. Furthermore, on the mountain are two *trees* 林林 (the tree of life and the tree of the knowledge of good and evil). We should also understand that the mountain is a place of worship, as we find worshiping *hands* 𝕀𝕀 .

mount

○ + ╲╱ + 林林 + 𝕀𝕀 = 燓

mountain   fire   trees   hands   burning
                          (worshiping)

In addition to the ⊢ and ⸘ (阝) forms of *mount* , (see p. 56), there are several other variations of this radical: ⸘ (B)[9], ⸘ (B)[10], ⸘ (B)[11]. Each of these symbols designates three *mouths, persons* ⸘ , ⸘ , ⸘ on the mount. (Again, notice the "blackening" of two of the symbols, indicating "holy.") Now let us examine the character *to descend* ⸘ (B)[12] (降). We recognize the "blackened, holy" feet ⸘ , indicating *to rest, stop* coming down to the holy *mount* ⊢ . Would this not tell us that the *mount* ⊢ is God's resting place?

descend

Once more in *mount* ⊢ we observe a reference to the three persons of the Godhead. From the Hebrew Scriptures we learn that the one great God of creation was actually manifest as the Father, Son, and Spirit. Do the ancient Chinese bear out the same idea?

The *Father* ⸘ (父) has already been described and

evidently took part in the creation of Adam and Eve. Examine the character meaning *to be, exist, possess*  (B) [13] (有). From the *Father's* extended hand appears the radical *flesh* (月), which we learned (pp. 42-43) symbolized the first couple.

to be, exist, possess

The Spirit of God was also mentioned at the time of creation in the Hebrew Scriptures:

> In the beginning God created the heaven and the earth. And the earth was without form, and void; and darkness was upon the face of the deep. And the Spirit of God moved upon the face of the waters.[14]

Compare this further description of the Spirit's activity in life and death:

> When You take away their breath,
>   they die and return to the dust.
> When You send Your Spirit,
>   they are created,
>   and You renew the face of the earth.[15]

We discover here that the "breath of life" is given by God's Spirit; when it is withdrawn, death occurs. So when Adam was formed from the dust of the ground and God breathed into his nostrils the breath of life, it was God's Spirit that gave the life.

> Then the Lord God took some soil from the ground and formed a man out of it; He breathed life-giving breath into his nostrils and the man began to live.[16]

Spirit

The very character for *Spirit* (S) [17] (靈) is most enlightening regarding the nature of God, so let us dissect it. First,

61

we find *God* ⊤ on the mountain ⌒ where the river of life is represented by *water* ᵈᵈ descending. Observe especially the three *mouths, persons* ᵛᵛᵛ , again suggesting the three persons of the Godhead. God is a *worker of magic* 巫 (s)[18] (巫) in His creative activity. *God* ⊤ (示) ended His *work* 工 (B)[19] (工) with the creation of Adam and Eve. *God* ⊤ and the two other *persons* ⌒ of the Godhead form the *Worker of Magic* 巫 .

$$⊤ + ⌒ + 工 = 巫 + ᵛᵛᵛ + 雨 = 靈$$

God	persons (two)	work	Worker of Magic	persons (three)	rain	Spirit

Examine a second form of *worker of magic* 巫 (o)[20] (巫), where ├ + ⊤ + ⊣ are clearly *God* ⊤ (示). Thus we find that the "God radical" is composed of ⊤ with ⌒, representing the Trinity, arranged around it (compare 示巫 , p. 31). Note an additional form of *Spirit* 靈 (B)[21] (靈), where 巫 has been replaced by the *God* radical 示 .

God's Spirit has been identified with the breath of life. How meaningful that an ancient figure for *breath* ☰ (☰ , p. 38) shows three strokes! We have just observed these three strokes ☰ in the radical *mount* ⊧ as well as in the *God* radical 示 . Recall, too, that ☰ is equated with *mouths, persons* ᵛᵛᵛ , as in ⊧ *mount*. Thus, it would seem conclusive that the three strokes ☰ also represent the three persons of the Trinity and, consequently, God's presence. Both Hebrew and Chinese sources disclose that the breath of life was given by God (the

(margin) 巫 *worker of magic*

(margin) 工 *work*

(margin) ☰ *breath*

(margin) 示 *God radical*

Trinity). Examine a second form of *breath* ≒ (B)22 (气), which likewise depicts the holy mountain ⌐.

A character indicating *perfect* 乐 (O)23 (全) portrays the combined *God* T and *breath* (Trinity) ≡ symbols, emphasizing God's *perfection*. The shape of 乐 suggests the *fountain* 巾 (p. 51).

$$ \text{T} \quad + \quad ≡ \quad + \quad 巾 \quad = \quad 乐 $$

| God | breath (Trinity) | fountain | perfect |

breath

perfect

We may well stand amazed at the knowledge of the venerable Chinese concerning the mystery of the Godhead. From the character 宗 (B)24 (宗), indicating *religion, belief in,* and *ancestral,* we may gather that the original religious beliefs of the Chinese centered about the Triune *God* 示 of heaven. They surely must have known that their ancestral religion and the faith of the very first *home* ⌐ (宀)—Adam and Eve's— was a belief in ShangTi. Apparently, the Chinese patriarchs wanted to preserve forever precious knowledge regarding China's original God, as they perceived Him, with their concept of the Trinity.

religion,
belief in,
ancestral

In an early form of *home* 家 (O)25 (家), under the *roof* ⌐ (宀) is depicted the symbol that we have interpreted as indicating God 才 (予, see discussion, p. 54). In a second ancient form, 家 (B)26 (家), we observe that, in the beginning, God was the head of the home. This figure 家 portrays *God, heaven* 天 (天) as well as the *Father* 父 (父).

home

天 + 丬 + 冂 = 宂
God (heaven)   Father   roof   home

It happens that in the evolution of the character for *home,* we find a duplication of what has happened in the homes of China. In a later form, 宂 (U) [27], the God of heaven is missing—forgotten! Only the ancestral *pair* 宀 + 丬 remain. Even later, it is a *pig* 豕 under the roof to symbolize a *home* 家 . What a travesty! Here the Chinese scribes made terrible mistakes in transcribing this character.

Unfortunately, the first close relationship between ShangTi and His beloved human couple changed. This separation of Adam and Eve from God, as well as for the reason for this deviation, we will find distinctly reflected in the pictographs of the next chapters.

7

Invader in the Garden

The Master said,
"Without recognizing the ordinances of Heaven,
it is impossible to be a superior man.
"Without an acquaintance with the rules of propriety,
it is impossible for the character to be established.
"Without knowing the force of words,
it is impossible to know men."
　　　　　　Confucian Analects, xx, iii

Shen
(God)

There is no doubt that a tender relationship existed originally between ShangTi (Shen) and people! This loving bond is shown by a further style of writing *Shen* (God) (B) [1] (神). The *couple* (⺈ + ⼁, the second *person* being upside down) is seen cleverly united in the symbol. How this first couple must have enjoyed and looked forward to conversation with and *instruction* (中) from their Creator God, who desired to be identified so intimately with them that they became a part of His name!

instruction

In the character *to be wedged between* 夾 (0)² (夾), this close relationship is quite obvious, for we recognize God, as a great, noble Being, with arms outstretched 大 , wedged between Adam and Eve, 人 + 人 .

wedged between

大   +   人   人   =   夾

noble Being (God)   two persons   to be wedged between

Sad events took place that destroyed these ties, separating Adam and Eve from their kind and beneficent Creator. In their many talks together, ShangTi had *instructed* 中 (中) Adam and Eve concerning an enemy, a mighty angel called Lucifer. This angel had rebelled against God's fair government of love in heaven.

Scenes of what took place regarding Lucifer in heaven are recorded by inspiration in the Hebrew Scriptures:

This is what the Sovereign Lord says:

> "You [Lucifer] were the model of perfection,
>   full of wisdom and perfect in beauty.
> You were in Eden,
>   the garden of God [in heaven]. ...
> You were blameless in your ways
>   from the day you were created
>   till wickedness was found in you. ...
>
> So I drove you in disgrace from the mount of God,
>   and I expelled you, O guardian cherub,
>   from among the fiery stones.
> Your heart became proud
>   on account of your beauty,
> and you corrupted your wisdom

because of your splendor.
So I threw you to the earth."[3]

Again, we learn more of Lucifer, the morning star, from the Hebrew Scriptures:

> How you have fallen from heaven,
>   O morning star, son of the dawn!
> You have been cast down to the earth....
> You said in your heart,
>   "I will ascend to heaven;
> I will raise my throne
>   above the stars of God;
> I will sit enthroned on the mount of assembly,
>   on the utmost heights of the sacred mountain.
> I will ascend above the tops of the clouds;
>   I will make myself like the Most High."[4]

Lucifer was not satisfied with his highest position among the angels. He wanted to be a god himself. He was consumed by jealousy at the creative power of ShangTi (Shen) in the formation of our earth. So he inspired a mass discontent among the angels of heaven. Lucifer spread false accusations against ShangTi, saying that God was a cruel tyrant. As a result, one-third of the angels of heaven joined Lucifer (also called Satan and the devil) in this rebellion. We turn once again to the record of the Hebrew people:

> Now war arose in heaven, Michael and his angels fight-
> ing against the dragon; and the dragon and his angels
> fought, but they were defeated and there was no longer
> any place for them in heaven. And the great dragon
> was thrown down, that ancient serpent, who is called

the Devil and Satan, the deceiver of the whole world—
he was thrown down to the earth, and his angels were
thrown down with him.[5]

There was no doubt that Lucifer would try to gain Adam
and Eve as his allies in his great controversy with ShangTi. We
should note in the above Hebrew narratives that "heaven,"
where God's throne is located on His sacred mountain, is also
metaphorically called "the Garden of Eden." So we learn from
this that the Garden of Eden that God prepared for Adam and
Eve in the newly created earth was actually a miniature of heaven
itself.

As ShangTi talked daily with Adam and Eve on His holy
mountain in the earthly Garden of Eden, He *invited* ✾ (B)[6]
(柬) them to *pick* and eat freely of the tree of life, for it
would give them immortality—everlasting life. At the *tree*
Ӂ , we find the two glorious sunlike persons ⊙ + ⊙ , whom
God had joined ⊕ in marriage. This tree must have represented the tree of life, because God had urged and invited them
to pick and eat from it.

On the other hand, He had forbidden access to the other
nearby tree in the middle of the garden, the tree of the knowledge of good and evil. Fruit from this tree was not theirs to
eat—or even to touch. God had imposed this one small, but
important, test upon them to prove their loyalty to Him as their
Creator and Benefactor.

Even before Eve was created on the sixth day of the first
week, God had cautioned Adam,

*invite,
pick*

"You are free to eat from any tree in the garden; but you must not eat from the tree of the knowledge of good and evil, for when you eat of it you will surely die."[7]

In the character *restrict, prevent, stop* (B)[8] (杜), the *tree* 木 must definitely refer to the forbidden tree, for in this character, we find the newly created *adult male* • of *dust* ⼟ to whom the restriction had been addressed. How very accurate the Chinese writing is, for Eve is not included in the character, as she had not yet been created on this day! She, of course, learned of the limitation later, for it applied to both of them.

restrict,
prevent,
stop

Yet another character, *to restrain, control* 困 (O)[9] (束), gives additional details regarding God's command. In 困 , we find a *mouth* ○ (口) for eating, superimposed on a *tree* 木 . The tree symbol slashing through the mouth radical suggests, "Don't eat; *control* 困 yourself!" This tree must have represented the forbidden tree, regarding which the first couple was warned they must control, or restrain, themselves from eating its fruit.

restrain,
control

Furthermore, the Chinese combined this character, 困 , with the *God* radical 丅 to express that God's command was the *law* 素 (O)[10] (索).

law

○	+	困	+	丅	=	素
mouth		tree		God		law

69

God's word and instruction, however lovingly given, were no less than an *imperial decree* (B)[41] (旨). The great *Being* ⌐, the Ruler of the universe, *speaks* ⊟ (日). And it was a death decree, should they fail to prove loyal to His kingdom of love.

imperial decree

God had surely been *straightforward* 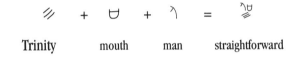 (B)[12] (侃) in His admonition to the couple. In this character, God is represented by ⫽ (see pp. 45, 62); ⼂ portrays *man,* and the *mouth* ⼝ depicts His talking.

straightfor-ward

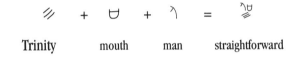

⫽	+	⼝	+	⼂	=	𝄃
Trinity		mouth		man		straightforward

One day, when Eve had become separated from her husband, she passed through the center of the garden. Suddenly she heard an unfamiliar voice. It was not Adam or ShangTi speaking. Who could it be? The voice seemed to come from the branches of the tree of the knowledge of good and evil. She *stopped* 休 (B)[13] (休), intrigued and curious. Eve, the *person* ⼂ (人), stood at the *tree* 木 of the knowledge of good and evil. There, sure enough, in its branches, was a beautiful serpent—and it was he who was talking!

stop

The talking serpent was a *foreigner* 夷 (B)[14] (夷) whose intent was to *exterminate, kill* 夷 the *noble man* 大 (Adam and Eve). In an oracle bone rendition of the same character, 夷 (O)[15] (夷), ⼂ has the appearance of a serpentlike, "snakey" man.

foreigner, exterminate, kill

$$⊂ \quad + \quad 大 \quad = \quad 夷$$

bent, curved   noble man   foreigner, to kill

But who was this, who, disguised as a serpent, addressed the unsuspecting Eve? It was none other than ShangTi's enemy, that old serpent Lucifer, the *devil* ⊕ (B)[16] (鬼), portrayed as a *garden* ⊕ *man* ꓶ . A second bronzeware depiction of the *devil,* ⊕ (B)[17] (鬼), is more specific. This time the *garden* ⊕ *man* ꓶ covers his *mouth* ⊔ . This has been well transcribed in the later pictograph ⊕ (S)[18](鬼), where ꓒ is a *man*, and ⌣ indicates *secret.* The devil was, indeed, a "secret garden man."

devil

$$⊕ \quad + \quad ⌣ \quad + \quad ꓒ(ꓒ) \quad = \quad ⊕$$

garden   secret   man   devil

⌣

*secret,
private*

The devil had waited for just this opportunity to approach Eve when she was alone. It was his plan to tempt her *privately* ⌣ (S)[19] (厶) with his persuasive argument. The devil began a conversation by asking, "Did God really tell you not to eat fruit from any tree in the garden?"[20]

Eve answered, showing that she understood exactly the restrictions God had made:

> "We may eat the fruit of any tree in the garden ... except the tree in the middle of it. God told us not to eat the fruit of that tree or even touch it; if we do, we will die."[21]

But the devil scoffingly answered, "You will not surely die."[22]

71

By this statement, the devil was completely negating what God had said. How interesting that the Chinese character for *negative, no, not* 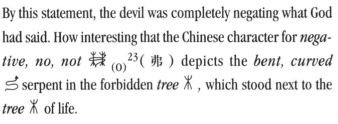 (O)[23] (弗) depicts the *bent, curved* 𝓈 serpent in the forbidden *tree* 朩 , which stood next to the *tree* 朩 of life.

negative, no, not

In his conversation with Eve, the devil continued:

> "For God knows that when you eat of it [the tree of the knowledge of good and evil] your eyes will be opened, and you will be like God, knowing good and evil."[24]

bent, curved

This was indeed a *magnanimous, expansive* (O)[25] (弘) offer. Again, the "serpentlike" man, the *bent, curved* 𝓈 (O)[26] (弓) *foreigner* ⟨ (the devil) speaks with his mouth 𝗏 (口).

magnani-mous, expansive

⟨	+	𝗏	=	𝓈𝗏
foreigner		mouth (speaks)		magnanimous, expansive

Unfortunately, Eve, the *person* ⼘ did not realize that this *man* ⼉ (人) in the *garden* ⊕ (田) was one to *dread, fear* 𝗅𝗈 (B)[27] (畏). Humanity's fate hung in the balance. Would Eve obey God or fall into the devil's snare?

dread, fear

8

The Lethal Bite

Follow with us the steps in the devil's deception of the woman who stood before the tree of the knowledge of good and evil. As she looked at the lovely tree, Eve was soon convinced that she need not fear death and that God was intentionally withholding good from them.

> The woman saw that the tree was good for food, that it was pleasant to the eyes, and a tree desirable to make one wise.[1]

She looked at the forbidden fruit and saw that it was "pleasant to the eyes," *beautiful* 媒 (o)[2] (媒). It was the *woman* 女 (女) who noted the beauty of the *fruit* 果 (o)[3] (果) on this *tree* 木 in the *garden* 田 . This character (果) must represent the forbidden fruit, for it also means *effect, consequence, result.*

beautiful

fruit, result, consequence

$$\text{果} \quad + \quad \text{女} \quad = \quad \text{媒}$$

fruit, result	woman	beautiful

The fruit was *desirable* (or *"covetable"*) 媒 (o)[4]

desire, covet

woman

(婪). Again, in this character, we find the *woman* 😊 facing one *tree* 木 , coveting the fruit, with her back to the second *tree* 木 . These characters record that it was not Adam, but the *woman* 😊 who initially distrusted ShangTi and disregarded His *warning*.

The Hebrew Scripture reports, "She took of its fruit and ate."[5] This sad waymark in the life of humanity is memorialized by another character for *beginning*, 始 (B)[6] (始), this time indicating the beginning of sin. Here is seen a *woman* 𠂉 *secretly* 厶 eating, symbolized by the *mouth* 凵 . There is no mistaking the intent in another stylized form, 始 (S)[7] (始), which shows the pictogram for *secretly, alone* 厶 (厶) dropping like a fruit into the open *mouth* 凵 (口) of the *woman* 𠂉 (女).

beginning

𠂉	+	厶	+	凵	=	始
woman		secretly		mouth (eating)		beginning

Eve had been no match for the wily serpent. She had been *weak* and *yielding* 弱 (O)[8] (弱). In this figure, we see her being molded by the "serpent man," the *foreigner* 𠂤 , Lucifer . She did not yet realize the consequence of her yielding to the suggestion of the devil, so she rushed to Adam with some of the fruit.

weak, yielding

> And she also gave some to her husband, and he ate.[9]

When Adam found that his lovely wife had disobeyed God's one command and eaten the forbidden fruit, he well-knew she was doomed to die. What was he to do? He quickly decided he *might as well* (O)[10] (索) join in Eve's disobedience. He no longer *restrained* (束) himself and reached with his *hand* ⅄ to take the fruit.

might as well

Both Adam and Eve had fallen into the devil's cleverly planned trap! They had become *disobedient* ⅄ (O)[11] (屰). Note the fallen, upside-down man. The *noble man* 大 had *stopped* (止) and *availed himself of* (B)[12] (乘)the forbidden *tree* 木 .

disobedient

$$大 + 止 + 木 = \text{(avail oneself of)}$$

noble man   stop   tree   avail oneself of

They had been tricked! They soon realized their understanding had not been broadened to their benefit, but to their great loss.

avail
oneself of

> Then the eyes of both were opened, and
> they knew that they were naked.[13]

As the glorious light signifying their sinless perfection and resemblance to God began fading, they discovered their nakedness. Hastily "they sewed fig leaves together and covered themselves."[14] Ashamed and naked, knowing ShangTi would soon be visiting them, they quickly made clothes of fig leaves. *Clothes* (O)[15] (衣) is a simple radical in which we find Adam, a *person* ，and Eve, a second *person* ，alone at the mountain . (Eve's origin from Adam's side is pictured.) But when we look at a later writing (U)[16] (衣) of *clothes*, we see the *couple* more clearly. In a matter of a few minutes, Lucifer had accomplished his goal of separating the human family from ShangTi. The devil substituted distrust and suspicion for loyalty and love to the heavenly Parent.

clothes

naked

A second word (see , p. 36) for *naked* (U)[17] (裸) designates *fruit* from the *Garden* ⊞ of Eden as a reason for the couple's nakedness.

⊞	+	朮	=	果	+	clothes	=	naked
garden		tree		fruit		clothes		naked

fruit

By their *disobedient* (弗) act of intentionally eating the fruit from the forbidden *tree* 朮 , they would forfeit access to the fruit from the tree of life which provided immortality as long as they regularly ate from it. God's plan was that they eat daily of the tree of life and live forever.

The time for ShangTi's *descent from heaven* (see p. 60) and daily visit had come. This interesting pictogram shows movement, for both of God's feet are depicted in contrast to a single foot, meaning *stop, rest* (p. 48). Also notice the downward direction of His glorious feet, indicating His descent. God came down to His sacred *mount* to meet with Adam and Eve. He, of course, already knew what had happened.

come

> That evening they heard the Lord God walking in the garden, and they hid from Him among the trees. But the Lord God called out to the man, "Where are you?"[18]

So Adam and Eve *came* (B)[19] (來) from behind a *tree* 朮 . The two *persons,* 人 + 人 , stood before their Creator, who looked at their hastily- put-together, fig-leaf garments and asked, "Did you eat the fruit that I told you not to eat?"[20]

ShangTi knew the *couple* 人 + 人 had made a lethal *stop*

76

ひ (止) in the *garden* 畾 (p. 37). They had *stumbled* and *fallen* (O)[21] (蹇) into the devil's snare.

stumble, fall

人 + 亻 + ひ + 畾 =

persons (two)   stop   garden   stumble, fall

Eve was especially *ashamed* (B)[22] (媿) to appear before God naked. It had been the *devil* who had tricked the *woman* .

garden

There followed a series of accusations and excuses with Adam, then Eve making their alibis:

> The man answered, "The woman you put here with me gave me the fruit, and I ate it."...
> She replied, "The snake tricked me into eating it."[23]

ashamed

God spoke first to Lucifer His enemy, who henceforth became known as "the old serpent," "the devil," and the "dragon":

> "I will put enmity [hatred]
> Between you and the woman,
> And between your seed and her Seed;
> He shall bruise your head,
> And you shall bruise His heel."[24]

In this curse put upon His foe, ShangTi pronounced, for the first time, a wonderful plan for humanity's ultimate salvation. Through later descendants of the woman Eve would eventually come the Savior, the promised *Seed* (O)[25] (子). In this writing of *seed, offspring* , observe the three strokes (see pp. 56, 62, 70), indicating God or His presence. It would seem that the ancient Chinese recognized a

seed, offspring

special, holy Seed, one who would crush and utterly defeat the devil and his angels. But in so doing, the Savior would suffer great agony on behalf of the guilty human race. This Savior was one of the Godhead, the "Son," who would one day come as a human being to earth.

Next, ShangTi addressed Eve:

> "I will greatly multiply
>   your sorrow and your conception;
> In pain you shall bring forth children;
> Your desire shall be for your husband,
> And he shall rule over you."[26]

Doubtless, God had originally intended the bearing of children to be a completely joyful experience. However, the bodily deterioration that womankind would suffer as the result of sin would no longer permit this. Pain would become the lot of women in childbirth. From this time also, the husband would rule over the wife. She would fall from her original position as his equal.

sorrow

Eve's *sorrow*  (O)[27] (楚) depicts again the site at the *trees* . The woman is represented by a *mouth* (口) for *eating* the fruit of the forbidden tree and also by a foot, with which she unwittingly *stopped* (止). A second form of *sorrow*, (O)[28] (楚), identifies a *noble person* (Eve) at the trees. Still a third rendition of *sorrow* (B)[29] pinpoints the act of stealing the fruit by a person's large arm reaching out toward one *tree* to grasp a *piece* (疌)

piece

of fruit. There is no mistaking Eve, standing with outstretched hand below the two trees, in this word for *sorrow* . But one must understand the original history, as did the venerable inventor of the written language, in order to interpret it correctly.

And what of Adam? His sorrow was also specific. Said God:

> "Cursed is the ground because of you;
> through painful toil you will eat of it
> all the days of your life....
> By the sweat of your brow
> you will eat your food
> until you return to the ground,
> since from it you were taken;
> for dust you are
> and to dust you will return."[30]

difficulty, trouble, worry

The character meaning *difficulty, trouble, worry,* (o)[31] (困), explains how eating from the forbidden *tree* 木 in the garden *enclosure* ☐ was the beginning of all people's difficulties and trouble. Now all Adam could do was *mourn* (B)[32] (吊) that he, *man* 勹 , had become entangled with the *bent, curved* 勹 serpent.

mourn

ShangTi had pronounced the sure penalty of *death* (o)[33] (死) for humanity's disobedience. God on His holy mount 阝 is depicted, pronouncing the death penalty for guilty *man* 勹 .

death

⊢	+	阝	+	勹	=	阝勹		
God		mount		man		death		

An inscription, *in consequence of, because, reason* (o)[34] (因), depicts a *noble man* 大 in the garden *enclosure* ☐ . Adam was that man, condemned to death because of disobedience. The fact that Adam and Eve lived on after their disobedience indicates that their death was ultimate

because, reason, consequence

and that they no longer possessed immortality. Spiritual death, however, was immediate, for they were cut off from God's presence and could no longer appear *face-to-face* (B)[35] (面) before Him. The *mount* 冂 in this character occurs with two other features: an *eye* (B)[36] (目), representing God's eye, and *ancient* 古 (B)[37] (古), depicting Adam, the *dust man* (土), given life by God's *breath, mouth* ⊔ . This pictogram thus portrays our ancient ancestor, Adam, in eye-to-eye, face-to-face communication with God on the holy mount.

face-to-face

ancient

$$\text{土} + \text{⊔} = \text{古} + \text{冂} + \text{◎} = \text{面}$$

dust(man)   mouth   ancient   mount   eye   face-to-face

Sin had now separated our first parents from their sinless God. They could no longer meet face-to-face. Because of his disobedience, God had declared that Adam would return to the ground from which he had been taken. Eve must suffer the same fate.

eye

How true the familiar Chinese saying: *"In the beginning, man's original character was virtuous"*:人之初性本善.

Unfortunately, humanity's perfect, sinless character was lost by a single willful act. Adam and Eve had eaten the forbidden fruit, knowing full well that they were disobeying the expressed command of their loving, kind Creator. They had listened to the words of the devil rather than God's warning. This resulted in their alienation from God, the source of all life. The separation of Adam and Eve from the Life-Giver meant death, an inescapable consequence. They had forfeited immortality. And they had brought it upon themselves.

80

9

A Costly Rescue Plan

Sorrowfully, God must now expel His beloved Adam and Eve from the Garden of Eden. The Hebrew record next states:

And the Lord God said, "The man has now become like one of us, knowing good and evil. He must not be allowed to reach out his hand and take also from the tree of life and eat, and live forever." So the Lord God banished him from the Garden of Eden to work the ground from which he had been taken. After he drove the man out, he placed on the east side of the Garden of Eden cherubim [angels] and a flaming sword flashing back and forth to guard the way to the tree of life.[1]

Interestingly, one of the ancient books of the Chou dynasty, records: "Because man sinned in ancient times, the God of heaven [天 帝] ordered Chung and Li to block up the way between heaven and earth."[2] Perhaps Chung and Li were the names given by the Chinese to the two angels on either side of Eden's gate.

So God expelled Adam and Eve from the garden. As they

gate

passed through the eastern garden *gate* (O)[3] (門), they realized this meant their exclusion from the life-giving tree of life and immortality. Note the hands and the barrier blocking the *gate* entrance. A *barrier, fence* (B)[4] (閑) had been set up, past which they could not go to eat from the *tree* of life. There were two angels (cherubim) guarding the way. Instead of the *hands* at the gate entrance, some ancient forms depict the "presence of God" at the *gate* (U)[5].

late, evening

The Chinese even pictographically record the time of day when the expulsion took place. It was *late, evening* (B)[6] (闌) when they passed through the *gate* . A *moon* (月) indicates the late hour, but in the distance is seen the *tree* of life to which the *couple* had previously been *invited* (p. 68).

The devil had claimed that God was a tyrant. If at this point ShangTi had abandoned Adam and Eve as hopeless rebels who could not even observe the smallest and simplest request possible, we might have to agree with the devil. But God did not leave His beloved Adam and Eve without hope. Already He had promised a Savior in the promised *Seed* of the woman. Now He wanted to explain more of the coming Savior's love for lost humanity.

ShangTi viewed the miserable fig leaf *clothes* (衣) Adam and Eve had fashioned for themselves (pp. 75-76). A costly and symbolic demonstration followed as the lives of innocent animals were sacrificed to provide skins to reclothe the sorrowing couple.

> The Lord God made garments of skin for Adam
> and his wife and clothed them.[7]

beginning

Never before had they witnessed the awfulness of death. Their beautiful animal friends were killed, thus symbolizing the death of God's sinless Son, One of the Godhead, who would come to earth as a human being and ultimately give His life for humanity.

This great act of clothing Adam and Eve with the skins of the sacrificial animals carries deep meaning and is memorialized in several Chinese characters. It was the *beginning* (O)[8] (初) of the plan of salvation for humanity. The symbolic *clothes* of skins for the guilty pair were provided only by the slaying of animals with a *knife* (O)[9] (刀).

knife

The new *robes* (O)[10] (袁) were a gift from *God* , here melded with His holy mountain . (Compare with 图, p. 51). Again we find the united *persons* who are symbolically *clothed* with the righteous character of the promised Son.

mountain + couple = clothes + God = robe

robe

Another character also using the significant radical *clothes* is *forgive, depend on, lean on* (O)[11] (依). Inserted into the radical is the great *Being* , God, whose provision of *garments* for the *couple* brought forgiveness and was meant to teach Adam and Eve that they needed to *depend on* Him for hope of salvation from eternal death.

forgive, lean on, depend on

to die

sheep

righteousness

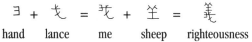

$$\wedge \quad + \quad \curlyvee \quad = \quad \wedge \quad + \quad \int \quad = \quad \wedge$$

mount   couple   clothes   Being (God)   forgive, depend on

Innocent animals had *to die* $\wedge_{(O)}$ [12] (卒) by Adam's *hand* ﻳ (手) so that God could provide *clothes* $\wedge$ for them. It is likely the creatures sacrificed were *sheep* 芏 $_{(B)}$ [13] (羊), for this animal above all others was to symbolize God's own Son who was later to be called "the Lamb of God who takes away the sin of the world."[14]

In the character for *righteousness* 羕 $_{(B)}$ [15] (義), we also find the *sheep* 芏 , like a garment, covering over *me* 找 $_{(B)}$ [16] (我). But "me" is composed of a *hand* ヨ (手) and *spear, lance* 弋 (戈)—which tells the story that I am responsible for the death of the *Lamb* 芉 , for my *hand* ヨ holds the killing instrument.

me

*lance,
spear*

$$\text{ヨ} \quad + \quad \text{弋} \quad = \quad \text{找} \quad + \quad \text{芏} \quad = \quad \text{羕}$$

hand   lance   me   sheep   righteousness

Originally, it was Adam whose sins were covered by the righteous *Lamb* 芏 of God. We discover this in the character *beautiful* 芺 $_{(O)}$ [17] (美), for the *noble man* 𠆢 , Adam, is pictographically portrayed. Eve, the *woman* 㐅 (女), was also included in some renditions of the character *beautiful* 羑 $_{(O)}$ [18] (美). When the Lamb covered their sins, they were indeed beautiful in God's eyes, for He could see only His sinless Son, represented by the *lamb* 芏 .

beautiful

Adam and Eve, now turned out of the garden, felt *alone* 單 $_{(B)}$ [19] (單). The conjoined *couple* ⵛ are depicted outside the *garden* ⊕ . It was time for them to *think, meditate* 川♣ (U) [20] (禪), not about their punishment, but about the goodness of *God* 川 , in spite of their ungrateful disloyalty. For God had provided *garments* 衮♣ (U) [21] (禪) for the unworthy *couple* ♈ , even though cast out of their *garden* ⊕ home.

alone

♈ + ⊕ = ♣ + 衮 = 衮♣
couple   garden   alone   clothes   garments

川♣ has an interesting secondary meaning of *leveling an area for an altar*. This was probably one of their first undertakings, for as they found themselves in *strange, unfamiliar* 畾♗ (O) [22] (異) surroundings, they felt their need of communion with God. Depicted outside the *garden* 田 is a kneeling figure 彡 with upraised hands, a characteristic posture of worship. A second form of this character *strange* 畾♗ (B) [23] reveals conjoined *hands* 彡彡 , which would suggest the hands of both worshipers are represented.

think, meditate

garment

彡彡(彡 + 彡) + 田 = 畾♗
hands   garden   strange, unfamiliar

We see them *seeking, praying to* 彡川 (B) [24] (覲) God. The first two *persons* ♈ are found outside the boundary of the *garden* 申 , while inside is God on the mount 彳 where the river 川 of life streams down the mountain side.

strange, unfamiliar

♈ + 申 + 卩 + ⌐ + 川 = 彡川
couple   garden   God   mount   river   to seek,

seek, pray to

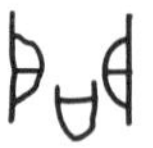
ask, inquire

The garden *gate* was the site where they came to *ask, inquire* (O)[25] (問) of God concerning their needs. The *gate* was also the place they came to *listen, hear* (S)[26] (聞) with the *ear* (耳) to what God had to say to them. The oracle bone writing of *listen, hear* (O)[27] (聞) shows the kneeling figure , which we have identified as Adam (see , p. 38) listening with both *ears* + . The *ear* (O)[28] (耳) in both the bronzeware and oracle bone writing appears to be a symbol of the holy *mountain* (山) in a vertical position. This would intimate that Adam's original instruction was given by God on the holy mount.

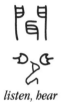

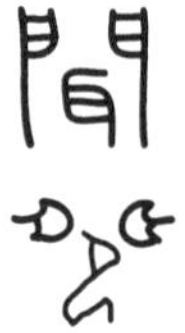
listen, hear

ear

The *gate* of Eden was evidently a place of glory, as indicated by the character *fiery* (O)[29] (閄), where a *fire* (火) is recognized.

> [God] placed cherubim [angels] at the east
> of the garden of Eden, and a flaming sword which
> turned every way.[30]

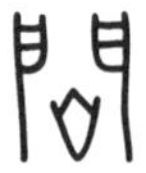
fiery

In another passage of Hebrew Scripture and at another time, God says, "I will speak with you … from between the two cherubim…."[31] Of God, the Scriptures also state, "Give ear, … You who dwell between the cherubim, shine forth!"[32] Could the flashing sword represent God's glorious presence there at Eden's gate, where the Chinese characters and tell us He communed with Adam and Eve?

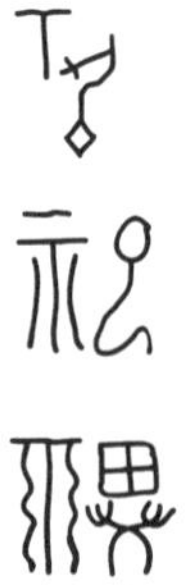
sacrifice

An unblemished *lamb* (B)[33] (羔), symbolizing the Savior to come, was sacrificed and burned at the gate. Animal *sacrifices* (O)[34] (祀) became an important part of their worship. The pictogram ⟨ reveals a *person* ⟨ bending in obeisance and offering with a *hand* ⟨ something to *God* ⟨. A bronzeware figure for the same character, *sacrifice* ⟨ (B)[35], portrays a *person* kneeling ⟨ before *God* ⟨. That the offering to God ⟨ was always made outside the *garden* ⊞ is quite obvious in yet another form of the same character, ⟨ (U)[36], in which we see the conjoined *hands* ⟨ as in *strange, unfamiliar* ⟨ above indicating two ⟨ + ⟨ worshipers.

sacrifice

An entirely different character for *sacrifice* ⟨ (B)[37] (祭) also has ancient roots. In this, we recognize the *hand* ⟨ serving *God* ⟨. Recall that the radical *flesh* ⟨ (⟨, pp. 43, 46, 61) represented two persons.

$$ ⟨ \quad + \quad ⟨ \quad + \quad ⟨ \quad = \quad ⟨ $$

flesh (two persons)　　　hand　　　God　　　to sacrifice

sacrificial animals

Oracle bone inscriptions of *sacrifice* ⟨ , ⟨ (O)[38] (祭) clearly reveal two *hands* ⟨ , ⟨ of two worshipers of *God* ⟨ , ⟨. Communion is depicted by the *mouth* ⟨.

ox, bullock

The sheep was not the only animal used in the worship of ShangTi, for the character *sacrificial animals* ⟨ (S)[38](犧) shows not only a *sheep* ⟨ but also a *bullock, ox* ⟨ (牛). The instrument for killing the animals was a *lance, spear* ⟨ (戈). Furthermore, we learn from this character that the animals must be *beautiful* ⟨ (秀), unblemished, or perfect. Only thus could they symbolize the sinless Son of God

beautiful, unblemished

to come. We can compare this Chinese pictograph with the instruction given by God to the Hebrews:

> "Take a bull calf for a sin offering, and a
> ram for a burnt offering, both without
> blemish, and offer them before the Lord."[40]

The character *sacrificial animals* 犧 has the same phonetic sound, "hsi," as *evening* ᗡ and *west* 畣. It would certainly suggest the word for "sacrificial animals" arose phonetically by association with the time of the ritual in the evening. *To sacrifice* 祀 (祀), on the other hand, also designates a time—9–11 A.M. Thus, it would seem, the early Chinese had two daily sacrifices: morning and evening. We can compare these Chinese pictographs with the instruction given by God to the Hebrews:

> One lamb you shall offer in the morning, and the
> other lamb you shall offer in the evening.[41]

The combined information gained from both the Chinese and Hebrew sources amplifies the story related in the Hebrew record regarding the sacrifices offered years later by Adam's first two sons, Cain and Abel:

> Now Abel kept flocks, and Cain worked the soil. In
> the course of time Cain brought some of the fruits of
> the soil as an offering to the Lord. But Abel brought
> fat portions from some of the firstborn of his flock.
> The Lord looked with favor on Abel and his offering,
> but on Cain and his offering he did not look with
> favor. So Cain was very angry, and his face was
> downcast. [42]

Cain was not bringing a proper sacrifice, and God would

not accept it. Cain had a rebellious spirit. So, in a fit of jealousy, because Abel's offering of a lamb had been accepted, he killed his brother.

The Chinese record this act of murder in the character *cruel, violent, fierce* 兇 (0)[43] (兇). We see Cain pictured as the *elder brother* 兄 (兄), who is taking hold of his younger brother, Abel 人 (人). Note that there is a *mark* ✕ on Cain, for in the Hebrew Scriptures it is recorded:

cruel, fierce, violent

> And the Lord put a mark on Cain, lest
> any who came upon him should kill him.[44]

When the Lord drove Cain from that place to become a fugitive in the earth, it is written that "Cain went out from the Lord's presence."[45] He no longer worshiped at the *gate* of Eden, where "God's presence" was manifested. Cain and his wife (his sister) became the ancestors of a rebellious race who hated God.

elder brother

But there have been those throughout the history of the earth who honored the God of heaven. It was these who kept alive a knowledge of Him and His wonderful plan for the salvation of all people. The Hebrews were one of these people, worshiping El Shaddai (p. 26). It appears that the ancient Chinese were other believers in the Creator, whom they called ShangTi.

Although the significance of ShangTi has been largely lost today in China, this sacred history of earth's beginnings was carefully recorded for all time in ancient Chinese pictographic and ideographic writing. This cryptic information has been awaiting recovery, so that both oriental and occidental peoples might have confidence in ShangTi (El Shaddai) as the God of the universe!

10

Unraveling a Confucian Puzzle

The new site for the worship of ShangTi was at the east gate of the Garden of Eden. This we learn from the Chinese characters and also from the Hebrew record, which reads:

> He drove out the man; and at the east of the gardenof Eden he placed the cherubim [angels], and a flaming sword which turned every way, to guard the way to the tree of life.[1]

The radical *gate* ▷◁ , ⌐⌐ (p. 82) shows not only God's *hands* ϶Ϛ (compare ⅏ p. 31, p. 35; ⟨ , p. 35), but also His presence ⅋ (⌐ , p.56; ⟝ , p. 63; 朩 p. 62) as well. The *gate* became a new holy place.

The original *place* ⌐⌐ (p. 56) of worship was on the *mountain* ⌐ (compare ⍦ , ⌐ , pp.59-60). That site or *place* was the holy hill where Adam and Eve, in their original sinless state, could *meet* (0)[2] (見) God face-to-face, eye-to-*eye* ⌀ (目), on bended knee Ϛ as worshipers. Note how ingenious this pictogram of *eye* ⌀ is, for the iris is actually the

meet

eye

*boundary,
border*

*rejoice, give
thanks to*

*grasp, take
hold of*

sun, glorious person ☉ , with the pupil being the *flame of fire* ˙ . This time, the *glorious person* ☉ represents God.

After Adam and Eve had been expelled from Eden, a *boundary, barrier* ⟊ (p. 82) had been set up at the gate to keep the first couple from the tree of life. The new location for worship, therefore, was at the garden *boundary, border* 𐤀 (O)[3] (圍). There are a number of oracle bone renditions for this character. Two have been selected in order to more accurately arrive at its meaning. In 𐤀, the worshiper is quite obvious as ⼄ . God is represented by 大 , the legs of which are melded with the legs of the *disobedient* ⼂ noble man. The second character for *border,* 𐤀 (O)[4] (圍), does not show the worshiper at the border of the garden *enclosure* □ , but a communication, indicated by a *mouth* ⼐ at the top of the God figure, as 大 .

A second *noble man* 大 (also called the Second Adam, the Savior) was to come and take the place of the first disobedient Adam. Therefore, all people can *rejoice* and give *thanks to* ⽂ (O)[5] (幸) the Savior, the second Adam. When the kneeling figure ⼄ is added, as 𐤀 (O)[6] (執), the new character means *grasp, take hold of.* All who desire to be saved from eternal death must *take hold of* 𐤀 the Savior. Finally, by placing this action at the *border* 𐤀 of Eden, we find depicted the original answer to Adam and Eve's plight.

Eden's gate was now the border or boundary past which they were prevented from going by the presence of the cherubim angels. There are many characters meaning *border*

92

or *boundary*. All have the same reference, the border of the Garden of Eden, more specifically, at the east gate.

The character meaning *frontier (border) gate* and also *to close, shut,*  $_{(O)}$[7] (關) shows two *persons* ⻊ + ⻊ , resembling *God* 夭 (天). These two ⻊⻊ stand at the *shut border gate* . Examine also an additional interpretation of the same character,  $_{(S)}$[8], which indicates a communication, *mouth* ▽ (口), at the *gate* ⌐ (門) between *two persons* ∴ ᠪ (compare , p. 46) and *God* ⊤ . The fact that God and the couple ᠪ are joined suggests a renewed close relationship between them. The upraised *hand* ⼹ portrays worship.

border gate, close, shut

$$\underset{\text{God}}{\top} + \underset{\text{two}}{\cdots} + \underset{\text{person(s)}}{᠔} + \underset{\text{gate}}{\sqcap} + \underset{\text{mouth}}{\triangledown} + \underset{\text{hand}}{⼹} = \underset{\text{border gate}}{}$$

A third character for *border* $_{(S)}$[9] (畔) portrays Adam, a *person* ⼛ , bowing outside the *garden* 田 , where "God's presence" ⼳ is manifested. A secondary, rather archaic, meaning of this symbol is *to come before God.*

boundary, border, to come before God

This is somewhat similar to the character *border, boundary* $_{(S)}$[10] (界) where *two* ⼁ + ⼁ *persons* ⼛ are once more found outside the *garden* 田 .

border

How amazing that there are so many Chinese characters for border, each of them denoting the border of Eden: the *garden* 田 , the garden *enclosure* □ , the *gate* ⻊⻊ , or in yet another, the holy mountain *border* $_{(S)}$[11] (際)! This is not difficult to interpret.

border

$$ \text{夕} \;+\; \text{尸} \;+\; \text{示} \;=\; \text{祭} \;+\; \text{阝} \;=\; \text{祭阝} $$

flesh	hand	God	sacrifice	mount	border
(two persons)					

Therefore, the *mount* 阝 itself, as it rose majestic and beautiful in the center of the garden, must have indicated the *border* 祭阝 of Eden where the sacrifice took place.

We may conclude that this daily service outside of Eden's east gate, was the Border Sacrifice initiated by ShangTi Himself. After Adam and Eve were driven from the garden, they could ask forgiveness for sin by a symbolic animal sacrifice at the border or gate of the Garden of Eden. The Border Sacrifice at Eden's closed gate looked forward to the sacrifice of the *"Seed* 夕 *of the woman"* (p. 77) on behalf of all the descendants of Adam.

We should not get the idea of a bloodthirsty god, demanding appeasement. Far from it, God was to sacrifice His own Son for the benefit of humanity who were under the death penalty. Of God, the Hebrew writings make clear:

> You do not delight in sacrifice, or I would bring it;
> You do not take pleasure in burnt offerings.
> The sacrifices of God are a broken spirit;
> a broken and contrite heart,
> O God, You will not despise.[12]

The great philosopher Confucius was a worshiper of ShangTi, a God whom he knew not. Although he used his influence to preserve the purity of the worship services to the "Heavenly Ruler," Confucius himself did not understand the ancient system of sacrifice that took place each year at the border of his country. In the Border Sacrifice, recall that the emperor alone took a young, unblemished bull, slew it, and burned it upon an altar. The whole ceremony was accompanied by music and recitations to ShangTi (some of which have been quoted in the first three chapters of this book). The emperor concluded the service by bowing low before the sacrificial altar in worship of ShangTi.

We might digress momentarily to learn a bit about the ancient sage Confucius, who stands as perhaps China's last guardian of original truth—dimmed almost to extinction in his day.

In the *Confucian Analects,* snatches of information paint a beautiful picture of the faith and integrity of this noble man:

> The Master said,
> "At fifteen, I had my mind bent on learning.
> At thirty, I stood firm.
> At forty, I had no doubts.
> At fifty, I knew the decrees of Heaven.
> At sixty, my ear was an obedient organ for the
> reception of truth.
> At seventy, I could follow what my heart desired,
> without transgressing what was right."[13]

Recall that *Heaven* 大 (p. 35), for the early Chinese, was a synonym for their God, ShangTi. Confucius' humility shines forth in these additional quotations:

> The Master said, "The sage and the man of perfect
> virtue;—how dare I rank myself with them? It may
> be simply said of me, that I strive to become
> such without satiety, and teach others without
> weariness."[14]

> The Master said, "When I walk along with two others, they may serve me as my teachers. I will select their good qualities and follow them, their bad qualities and avoid them."[15]

> The Master said, "Heaven *[T'ien, God]* produced the virtue that is in me."[16]

Confucius had always been interested in the ancient sacrifice custom, realizing there must be an important significance to the ceremony. Therefore, he spent much time researching into its true meaning. But finally Confucius had to admit,

> "He who understands the ceremonies of the sacrifices to Heaven and Earth ... would find the government of a kingdom as easy as to look into his palm!"[17]

In Confucius' day, about 500 B.C., at least 1700 years had already passed since the dynastic rule of China was established. The first rulers, it appears, understood the religious principles that had been handed down by word of mouth from the time of creation. The ancient sage who had invented the written language also had true concepts of the history of the world. He recorded this knowledge for all time in his ideographic characters. The Hsia and Shang dynasties had passed, and now, during Confucius' lifetime, the famed Chou dynasty was ruling China. Because of the long passage of time, therefore, a true knowledge of ShangTi had already been lost. The Border Sacrifice, part of the worship of ShangTi, had survived in name only to become a mysterious ritual, a national custom of unknown significance and origin.

As we have briefly reviewed the history of Adam and Eve, we found that their unfortunate act of disobedience and dis- loyalty meant the death sentence. But ShangTi had proposed to ransom them by sending a Savior to be born as the *Seed* 🌾 of the woman. In the plan, this Savior would crush the head of the serpent, that old enemy of God, the devil. However, the Savior Himself would be bitten in the heel. What did this mean?

When Adam and Eve left their beautiful garden home, ShangTi had lovingly provided garments of skins for them. These *robes* 衣 (p. 33) made necessary the death of innocent sacri- ficial animals, likely *sheep* 羊 , to cover their nakedness. The *Lamb* 羔 (s)[18] (羔) (note the *fire* 火 beneath the *sheep* 羊, indicating the sacrifice) was another symbol of the com- ing Savior. The sacrifice of this animal was to represent the Savior's death and payment for their sentence, "You will surely die." The sinless Savior would substitute His life for sinful humanity.

lamb

"You will not die" had been the devil's promise to Eve. Who would be right, ShangTi or the devil? Death has come upon all people, from Adam's son, Abel, the first to die, to our very day.

God had told Adam he would return to dust. Death is the opposite of creation, as we leaned in a previously quoted He- brew text:

> When You take away their breath,
>   they die and return to the dust.
> When You send Your Spirit,
>   they are created.[19]

Compare also:

When his breath departs, he returns to his earth;
on that very day his plans perish.[20]

But there is hope that the dead will live again. This is ShangTi's wonderful plan of salvation. God's own Son would one day be born on earth as the *Seed* 𜵟 of the woman, live a sinless life among people, and give His life for all people who allow themselves to be covered by the *righteousness* 羲 (p. 84) of this heavenly sacrifice. There will be a day when all the righteous dead will live again according to this Hebrew record:

> And many of those who sleep in the dust of the earth shall awake, some to everlasting life, and some to shame and everlasting contempt. And those who are wise shall shine like the brightness of the firmament; and those who turn many to righteousness, like the stars for ever and ever.[21]

In Confucius' day, that supreme sacrifice had not yet been made. The promised Seed of the woman, the Savior of all humanity, had not yet come. But about 200 years before the time of Confucius, a Hebrew prophet had looked far down into the future, writing in past tense as though the event had already happened. Listen to this highly descriptive and detailed picture that he related about the Savior to come:

> "Who would have believed what we now report?
>   Who could have seen the Lord's hand in this?
> It was the will of the Lord that His servant
>   grow like a plant [Seed] taking root in dry ground....
> We despised Him and rejected Him;

He endured suffering and pain.
No one would even look at Him—
    we ignored Him as if He were nothing.
But He endured the suffering that should have been ours,
    the pain that we should have borne.... .
Because of our sins He was wounded,
    beaten because of the evil we did.
We are healed by the punishment He suffered,
    made whole by the blows He received.
All of us were like sheep that were lost,
    each of us going his own way.
But the Lord made the punishment fall on Him,
    the punishment all of us deserved.
He was treated harshly, but endured it humbly;
    He never said a word....
He was arrested and sentenced and led off to die,
    and no one cared about His fate.
He was put to death for the sins of our people.
He was placed in a grave with evil men,
    he was buried with the rich,
even though He had never committed a crime
    or ever told a lie."
The Lord says,
"It was My will that He should suffer;
    His death was a sacrifice to bring forgiveness....
    and through Him my purpose will succeed.
After a life of suffering, He will again have joy;
    He will know that He did not suffer in vain.
My devoted servant, with whom I am pleased,
    will bear the punishment of many
    and for His sake I will forgive them.
And so I will give Him a place of honor,
    a place among great and powerful men.
He willingly gave His life
    and shared the fate of evil men.
He took the place of many sinners
    and prayed that they might be forgiven."[22]

In Confucius' day, the promise had not yet been fulfilled; the time was still in the future for ShangTi's purposes to be realized.

The Han dynasty followed the famed Chou dynasty of Confucius' era. During the reign of Emperor Ai 哀帝 [23] (and perhaps his name was prophetic in meaning, "to pity, to sympathize with"), a son was born to a humble peasant couple, Joseph and Mary. They lived in a land far-distant from China. On a map, you may locate the country of Israel (today, much in the news) to the east of the Mediterranean Sea. This was the ancient land of the Hebrews, whose venerable Scriptures we have been comparing with the Chinese character writing. In a small town of Bethlehem in the province of Judea, an event of great importance to the whole world took place. But many strange things happened simultaneously with the birth of the special baby.

11

The Seed
of the Woman

The first in a series of strange events was the appearance of
a heavenly angel to a lovely young woman, Mary, with an important message. Mary was looking forward to her approaching marriage with Joseph. Both were descendants of King David,
in the royal Judean line. But it had been centuries since a Judean
king had ruled over Israel. Indeed, at that time (about 2,000
years ago), their nation was under the tyrannical rule of Rome.
Joseph was, instead of a prince, a humble carpenter in the
town of Nazareth.

The visit of an angel was a rare event of great honor, and
the heavenly messenger put aside Mary's fears by saying:

> "Don't be afraid, Mary; God has been gracious to
> you. You will become pregnant and give birth to a
> son, and you will name Him Jesus. He will be great
> and will be called the Son of the Most High God.
> The Lord God will make Him a king, as His ancestor
> David was ... His kingdom will never end!"[1]

Perplexed, Mary spoke to the angel, "I am a virgin. How, then, can this be?"[2]

> The angel answered, "The Holy Spirit [one member of the Godhead] will come on you, and God's power will rest upon you. For this reason the holy child will be called the Son of God" [a second member of the Godhead].[3] (See chapter 3.)

Mary responded, "I am the Lord's servant, ... may it happen to me as you have said."[4]

An angel also visited Joseph, reassuring him:

> "Joseph, descendant of David, do not be afraid to take Mary to be your wife. For it is by the Holy Spirit that she has conceived. She will have a son, and you will name Him Jesus—because He will save His people from their sins."[5]

So Joseph took Mary as his wife, but he had not consummated the marriage. A few months later, a great census was being taken throughout the Roman Empire. All were required to register in the hometown of their family's ancestral leader. Thus Joseph and Mary journeyed to Bethlehem, the ancient town of their ancestor, King David.

Bethlehem, they found upon their arrival, was so crowded with travelers that there were no empty inn rooms. The best they could do was to find a sleeping place on the sweet-smelling hay in a barn. It was under these humble conditions that Jesus, the long-awaited "*Seed* � of the woman," was born to this poor peasant couple.

The human family had known predictions of a promised Savior since Adam and Eve were expelled from the Garden of

Eden. Yet how many expected Him at this time? In the Hebrew sacred writings, there were many prophecies foretelling of Jesus' coming to earth. Daniel, a prince and prophet living as a captive in Babylon during Confucius' own lifetime, had written of the time when the Savior would appear. But only a few had bothered to study the Hebrew Scriptures sufficiently to learn when this might be. These faithful ones knew His coming must be soon. Among the expectant believers were simple shepherds who often talked of the Savior and what His coming would be like. As these herdsmen were watching their flocks in the countryside one night, an angel appeared to them also, joyously announcing:

> "Don't be afraid! I am here with good news for you, which will bring great joy to all the people. This very day in David's town your Savior was born—Christ the Lord! And this is what will prove it to you: you will find a baby wrapped in cloths and lying in a manger."[6]

Then appeared to the amazed shepherds a great host of angels singing and rejoicing. The angels directed the shepherds to where Mary, Joseph, and the Baby were—not to a palace, but to an animal shed.

The child had other visitors as well. Three wise men arrived from the Orient. They too had studied the prophecies of the Hebrew Scriptures and had seen a beautiful, moving star arise in the east. They had learned that a special star would be seen in the heavens to announce the birth of a Savior. Therefore, they followed the star a great distance. The star led them to Jerusalem, where they inquired of the ruler, Herod, the whereabouts of the child born to be the King of the Jews. Herod was greatly upset. He called together the chief priests and teachers of the people to ask where the Savior was to be born. They read for him the prophecy that had been written hundreds of years before:

> "Bethlehem Ephrathah, you are one of the smallest towns in Judah, but out of you I will bring a ruler for Israel, whose family line goes back to ancient times."...

> When He comes, He will rule His people with the strength that comes from the Lord and with the majesty of the Lord God Himself. His people will live in safety because people all over the earth will acknowledge His greatness, and He will bring peace.[7]

Herod was so disturbed by this word that he determined to destroy the child who would possibly depose him from his throne. Without revealing his evil intentions, Herod said to the wise men, "Go and make a careful search for the child; and when you find Him, let me know, so that I too may go and worship Him."[8]

Once more the star appeared, and the oriental sages followed it to the very place where Jesus was resting. The three visitors from the east entered the dwelling and knelt before the child. They gave gifts of gold, frankincense, and myrrh, which they had brought with them. These men were then warned in a dream not to return to Herod, so they left for their own country by another route.

Again an angel appeared to Joseph with the warning to take his family immediately to Egypt. This he did—and none too soon, for Herod sent his soldiers with the order to kill all the boys of two years and younger in the region of Bethlehem. The gifts of the oriental wise men served to support the family while in Egypt, where they stayed until the death of the wicked king Herod. Then they returned to Nazareth.

When Jesus was 12 years old, Joseph and Mary took Him with them to the yearly Passover Festival in Jerusalem. On their way home, they suddenly realized the boy was not with their company of travelers. They returned to Jerusalem and spent the next three days frantically searching for Him. At last they decided to look in the temple, and there they heard His voice. He was

> sitting with the Jewish teachers, listening to them and asking questions. All who heard Him were amazed at His intelligent answers.... His mother said to Him, "Son, why have You done this to us? Your father and I have been terribly worried trying to find You."
>
> He answered them, "Why did you have to look for Me? Didn't you know that I had to be in My Father's house?" But they did not understand His answer."[9]

Jesus identified Himself with God, calling Him "Father," and the temple He named as "God's house." Was Jesus inquiring of the priests about the significance of the sheep sacrifices that He had witnessed in the temple? We do not know. He returned then to Nazareth with His parents.

Nothing more is known of the childhood and youth of Jesus, who grew to manhood working in Joseph's carpenter shop in Nazareth. One short statement summarized this period of His life: "The child grew and became strong; He was full of wisdom, and God's blessings were upon Him."[10] We do know that His life from the beginning was empowered by the Holy Spirit within Him, so that He lived a life totally without sin. No other person on earth has ever been able to do this.

At the age of 30, Jesus left the carpenter's bench and went to Jerusalem. Shortly thereafter, He was baptized in the Jordan River by His cousin John, who had become a famous preacher. Following the public baptism of Jesus, John announced, "There is the Lamb of God, who takes away the sin of the world!"[11] Why did he specify this animal used as a sacrifice in the temple services? We will soon understand.

Jesus then began His work that He had come into the world to do. Immediately the devil came to Him with a series of grueling temptations, far worse than the simple temptation that had led Adam and Eve to disobey God. Satan was eager to overcome the Son of God in His vulnerable human form. But unlike Adam and Eve, Jesus overcame each test by relying upon the power that God gave Him. He did not separate Himself from the Father's ever-present help as Adam and Eve had. As a man, He also understood, from His knowledge of the Hebrew Scriptures, the truth about the war between God and Lucifer (Satan, the devil).

Jesus chose 12 ordinary men of various ages and

occupations to be His disciples. Several were fishermen; one was a tax collector. His righteous character, His forthright teachings, and His mastery of every situation attracted them. Jesus had great compassion, and as He passed from town to town, His fame as a great healer preceded Him. Sick people with every kind of hopeless disease were brought to Him. By divine miracles, He immediately brought all back to complete health and soundness of body and mind. Often after He had healed them, He said, "Your sins are forgiven; go and sin no more."

He taught about God's coming kingdom by telling stories with deep meaning, drawing illustrations from current happenings or from nature. His work for others was tireless. Yet He had enemies—the religious leaders. "How can this unlearned carpenter forgive sins? By what authority does He teach the people and especially forgive sins? Only God has the power and right to remove sin. How dare this mere man assume the authority that only God has!" So thought these men who tried over and over to trap Him in a misstatement, an untruth, an inconsistency of life or teaching.

Always Jesus showed the utmost wisdom and insight in dealing with them. He did not hesitate to point out their errors in a direct manner, which only further angered them.

On three occasions Jesus raised people from death to life again. One of those resurrected, a dear friend, had been dead and entombed for four days. Again the religious leaders attempted to discredit these acts as mere magic, done under the influence of the devil.

In spite of the controversy with these leaders, Jesus was popular and greatly loved by the common people. Some of them were convinced that He must be the long-awaited Savior, the Seed of the woman, sent from God. Jesus' public ministry lasted only three-and-a-half years, ending when one of His own disciples betrayed Him.

The day of the great, national yearly celebration, the Passover Feast, drew close. When 12 years old, Jesus had observed this event in Jerusalem with His parents. In commemoration of the Hebrews' deliverance from Egyptian slavery centuries before, the Passover was still annually kept. This had been not only a historical escape from bondage, but it had also symbolized the eventual release of God's people from the captivity of Satan and sin.

Under the guidance of God and the leadership of Moses, each Hebrew family that first Passover evening in Egypt had killed a lamb. They had been directed to wipe its blood over the doorways of their houses. This was a sign for God's destroying angel to *pass over* their houses, when the firstborn of all the Egyptians were to be slain. The lamb's blood was a sign that the Hebrew firstborn were to be saved from death in that crisis hour. Moreover, the Hebrews ate the flesh of the roasted lamb, but no bones in its body were to be broken. This entire epic bore deep symbolic meaning.

Since that time, the ceremony had been repeated each year with the sacrifice and eating of the Passover lamb. In Jesus' day, the Hebrews still conducted the ritual (in addition to the daily morning and evening lamb sacrifices in Jerusalem's temple). Lambs and oxen had been sacrificed from the time of Adam at Eden's border gate, pointing forward to this very time. Even in China, a yearly Border Sacrifice was conducted, though it significance was no longer understood.

On the evening before the Passover, Thursday night, Jesus called His 12 disciples together in the upper room of a house. While they all sat at a table, He "took a piece of bread, gave thanks to God, broke it, and said, 'This is My body, which is [broken] for you.'"[12] Then each of the men ate portions of the bread. Eating of the Passover lamb had also symbolized the body of Jesus, which was soon to be "broken."

Next, Jesus passed around sweet wine for each to drink, saying, "This is My blood, ... [which is] poured out for many for the forgiveness of sins. I tell you, I will never again drink this wine until the day I drink the new wine with you in My Father's Kingdom."[13] But the disciples failed at first to understand the deep significance of the service.

After leaving the room that evening, Jesus and His friends, except for one who had excused himself early, went to a garden to pray. However, sleep overcame all His followers, and Jesus alone prayed to the Father in heaven for strength to go through the ordeal He faced on behalf of all people.

While Jesus was still there in the garden, a noisy crowd approached and, from their midst, the missing disciple stepped forth and kissed Jesus. At this signal, Jesus was arrested and taken prisoner. Suddenly He was alone in the hands of an angry mob, for His disciples had fled. Now read once more the amazing details of the prophecy recorded over 500 years before regarding the events that were to occur this night (pp. 98-99). The time had come!

12

Resolving the Altar
of Heaven Mystery

It was before dawn on Friday morning. Jesus, with hands bound, was pushed and shoved through the dark and empty streets of Jerusalem toward the house of the high priest. A number of teachers of the law and other religious leaders had gathered in his home at this unusual hour. As an unofficial, assembled council, they attempted to find some crime of which to accuse Jesus, so that they could demand His death.

Many false witnesses came forward with lying statements. These seemed insufficient, until finally two men stepped up and reported, "This man said, 'I am able to tear down God's Temple and three days later build it back up.' "[1] Immediately the high priest demanded that Jesus reply to this accusation. When He remained silent,

> the high priest said to Him, "I charge You under oath by the living God: Tell us if You are the Christ, the Son of God."

> "Yes, it is as you say," Jesus replied, "But I say to all

of you: In the future you will see the Son of Man
sitting at the right hand of the Mighty One and
coming on the clouds of heaven."[2]

In horror, the high priest tore his priestly garments and
cried, "Blasphemy! This man claims to be God! You have just
heard Him. What do you think?"

They all answered, "He is guilty and must die!" So they spat
in His face and slapped and beat Him. They put Him in chains
and led Him off to the Roman governor, for the Jews could not,
by themselves, effect His execution, since they were under
Roman rule.

Next, Pontius Pilate, the Roman governor questioned Him,
"Are you the king of the Jews?" Jesus neither answered him
nor the many accusations being made by the religious leaders.
Puzzled, the governor declined to make a decision, sending
Him off instead to the local ruler over the region Jesus was
from. Having heard much about Jesus, the ruler hoped to see
Him perform some miracles. He asked Him many questions,
but again Jesus remained silent. Because Jesus did not respond
to their purposeless inquiries, the ruler and his soldiers treated
Him with contempt. In mockery, they put on Him a fine robe
and sent Him back to Pilate.

Now Pilate could no longer postpone his decision. He said
to the Jewish religious leaders, "I have not found Him guilty of
any of the crimes you accuse Him of. Nor did [the other ruler]
find Him guilty.... So I will have Him whipped and let Him
go."[3] But the gathering crowd cried out, "Kill Him!"

Pilate wanted to set Jesus free, and since it was the custom at Passover time to free whatever prisoner the crowd demanded be released, he asked them, "Shall I set free the criminal Barabbas or Jesus?" The crowd, influenced by the religious leaders, demanded Barabbas be freed and Jesus be put to death. When Pilate realized a riot might break out if he did not comply with the wishes of the people, he took some water and washed his hands before them saying, "I am not responsible for the death of this man! This is your doing!"[4]

So, through a great failure of justice, this noble man, the Son of God, was lashed by Roman whips until His back was torn and bleeding; a crown of thorns was placed on His head in ridicule. Blows to the head drove the thorns into His brow, until the blood streamed down His face. They spit on Him and then made Him carry His own heavy wooden cross, for crucifixion was the method of execution used by the cruel Romans. Calvary, the place of crucifixion, was on a small hill. When Jesus stumbled under the load, weak from the torture and abuse that had been heaped upon Him, a stranger from a foreign country was made to carry the cross for Him.

Calvary was located outside Jerusalem's gate. How important this fact is! The Bible relates:

> So Jesus also suffered outside the gate in order to sanctify the people through His own blood.[5]

Even as Adam's sacrifice of unblemished lambs had been made outside Eden's gate, so also the Lamb of God was offered outside of Jerusalem, the holy Hebrew city. This too was a fulfillment of the ancient Chinese Border Sacrifice, the "border" being Eden's gate, typifying Jerusalem's gate where the great sacrifice for all humanity was to be made.

Roman soldiers laid out Jesus on the cross, nailing His outstretched arms, as well as his feet, to the rough wooden cross beneath. They then unmercifully dropped the cross into a prepared hole in the ground, which caused the weight of His body to tear the flesh of His hands and feet into gaping wounds. He took all the abuse without an outcry. He even murmured, "Forgive them, Father! They don't know what they are doing."[6] The crosses of two thieves, scheduled for execution at the same time, stood on either side of the central cross where Jesus hung.

Picture the scene. Three crosses are silhouetted on a hill against a darkening sky. On the highest, central cross hangs the Son of God. As we see the Savior *hanging with outstretched, upraised arms,* held fast by the cruel nails through His hands, we remember a familiar figure Ψ . How many times have we seen symbols of ShangTi standing on the stylized mountain with arms upraised in blessing: 쥊 (p. 45); 圀 (p. 51); 㿷(p. 55); 㿯 (p. 55); 㿙 (p. 56); 㿴 (p. 83); 㿶 (p. 85)? What greater blessing is there than the sacrifice Jesus was making at that hour for all humanity?

It was 9 A.M., the time of the morning *sacrifice* 㿿 (pp. 86-87) of the lamb in the temple, when Jesus was hung upon the cross. He suffered anguish from terrible physical pain, but far worse, He bore the crushing sins of all humanity which were separating Him from God the Father. He cried out, "My God, My God, why have You forsaken Me?"[7]

As Jesus endured the pain and mockery of the cross, He was dying the sinners' death—that death which is a solitary one, without God. He died for lost humanity of all generations, from Adam and Eve's time—and yes, even into the future, to the end of time.

It was 3 P.M., the hour for slaying the *sacrificial animals* 犧牲 (p. 87) in the evening, when Jesus spoke His last words, "It is finished,"[8] and breathed His last. The sacrifice of the ages was complete. Every unblemished lamb or bull offered in the past had pointed forward to this very hour. It was the very moment in time and the act that had so puzzled the sage Confucius. The sacrificial death of Jesus had been represented by thousands of burning bulls offered by successive emperors of China at the annual Border Sacrifice. Even in our 20th century, this ancient rite was still being conducted at Beijing's Altar of Heaven.

All nature convulsed as its Creator died. There was a mighty earthquake. Strange things happened

> Then the curtain hanging in the Temple was torn in two from top to bottom. The earth shook, the rocks split apart, the graves broke open, and many of God's people who had died were raised to life. They left the graves, and after Jesus rose from death, they went into the Holy City, where many people saw them.[9]

The tearing of the magnificent curtain in the temple

indicated a completion of the sacrificial service there conducted. The Lamb of God, to whom all the temple services pointed, had been slain. Henceforth, all sacrifices would be meaningless. But in China, what had transpired outside the gates of Jerusalem was completely unknown. The emperors' slaying of the unblemished bull at the great Border Sacrifice continued year after year.

The reigning ruler of China at the time of Jesus' death was Emperor Kuang Wu 光武帝.[10] Perhaps his name, "The Hero of Light," was also prophetic. Many thousands of miles away from China, unbeknown to the Chinese, the world's greatest hero of all time had given His life for the world. Jesus never called Himself a hero, but He had said, "I am the light of the world.... Whoever follows Me will have the light of life and will never walk in darkness."[11] One of His disciples later said of Him, "That was the true Light which gives light to every man who comes into the world."[12]

A bold Roman soldier, not being certain whether Jesus had indeed died, thrust a spear into His side as He hung on the cross, and out flowed blood and water. His death, Jesus had promised, would mean *eternal* 永 (B)[13] (永) life for everyone who would believe that He truly was the Son of God. How appropriate that the inventor of Chinese writing, more than 2,000 years before, had written *eternal* 永 to resemble the flowing water of the *river* 川 of life! Not only that, but look closely and you will see God (Jesus) as a *man* 人 in the very center of 永, surrounded by an artistically arranged 永,

indicating "God's presence" (compare $\overline{\overline{\pi}}$, p. 62).

$$\wedge \quad + \quad \widehat{\wedge}\ (\mathscr{W}\ )\ =\ \widehat{\wedge}\wedge$$

a Man (Jesus)　　God's presence　　eternal

There is another clever ancient character picturing eternal life. It is beautifully inscribed in the bronzeware depiction of *long life* (B)[14] (壽). This pictogram once again portrays ShangTi as the *central* $\wedge$ (方) Being, forming also the holy mountain $\curvearrowright$ (compare , p. 55; , p. 55). This time the three persons of the Godhead are represented, not only by three pairs of upraised arms $\mathcal{Y}$, but also by the three *mouths, persons* arranged along the curving line descending from the sacred mount as the river of life $\supset$. Although only the Son of God suffered on the cross, this sacrifice was a precious gift to humanity from the whole Triune Godhead.

eternal

long life

> For God so loved the world that He gave His only Son, that whoever believes in Him should not perish but have eternal life.[15]

For Jesus' disciples, the darkest hour had come. They were not remembering Jesus' words pronounced at the last supper with Him in the upper room. They had eaten bread and drunk sweet wine, of which Jesus said, "This is My body" and "this is My blood, which seals God's covenant, My blood poured out for many for the forgiveness of sins."[16] They, instead, had built their hopes upon His becoming a king who would throw off the Roman rule. Even they did not then understand His true universal mission on behalf of all humanity around the earth, and not for Israel alone.

Two wealthy and heretofore secret friends and believers of

Jesus now came forward to claim His body. Not one bone of His body had been broken. If He had not died before sunset, the soldiers would have broken His legs to hasten His death. Recall that no bones of the Passover lamb were to be broken. Jesus was that lamb.

Those eminent men now wrapped His body in strips of cloth and placed Him in a new tomb, cut out of a rock, which had actually been purchased for one of them. A great stone was rolled before the opening. Roman guards posted at the request of the high priest watched the tomb to prevent His disciples from stealing away the body. The religious leaders remembered Jesus saying on a number of occasions that He would be resurrected on the third day: "Destroy this temple [My body], and I will raise it again in three days."[17]

The weekly seventh day of rest, commemorating God's original six days of work in creating the earth and all plant and animal life, was drawing on as the sun set in the western sky. This Sabbath, the world's Creator *rested* 𝄢 (止) in the tomb. He had accomplished for humanity His appointed mission of making possible the re-creation of each person's character through His own gift of *righteousness* 公義. How significant that this ideographic combination conveys the idea that *righteousness* is open to *all* 公 people, all the descendants of Adam!

> For just as all people die because of their union with Adam, in the same way all will be raised to life because of their union with Christ [Jesus].[18]

Very early on the third day after His death, the first day of the week, there was another earthquake. An angel descended from heaven and rolled back the great stone from the mouth of the tomb. The guarding Roman soldiers dropped to the ground as dead men at the dazzling brightness of the angel. Jesus stepped forth from the tomb—the resurrected Savior. The fallen "Temple of God" had indeed been restored in three days, according to His promise.

The risen Son of God appeared to His disciples and to many others on several occasions. At last, 40 days after His resurrection, He and His disciples walked past the garden where He had prayed the night of His arrest and on to the Mount of Olives.

> When He had led them out to the vicinity of Bethany, He lifted up His hands and blessed them. While He was blessing them, He left them and was taken up into heaven.[19]

Our final picture of Jesus, the Son of God, is of Him on the Mount of Olives, with upraised arms in blessing. It was the same posture ShangTi, from the very beginning, had taken on the holy mount when Adam and Eve *returned* 㡱 (p. 55) there to worship.

As His disciples watched, Jesus began to rise from the earth. An angel announced to the disciples: "This Jesus, who was taken from you into heaven, will come back in the same way that you saw Him go to heaven."[20] Today, 2,000 years later, we must seriously ponder: Does all this have meaning for me?

119

13

ShangTi's Last Promise

In the second chapter of this little book, the question was asked, "Where did we come from?" But there are other equally puzzling questions frequently contemplated by most individuals: "Why am I here?" "Is there more to life than this?" "Will I live again after this life?" In other words, "Where am I going?"

Jesus, the Son of God, said to His disciples while He was here on earth:

> "Do not be worried and upset.... Believe in God and believe also in Me. There are many rooms in My Father's house, and I am going to prepare a place for you. I would not tell you this if it were not so. And after I go and prepare a place for you, I will come back and take you to Myself, so that you will be where I am....
>
> "No one goes to the Father except by Me."[1]

In the Holy Bible, ShangTi's own book, we can read more about the place where Jesus went and is still living today. The

Bible describes it as a beautiful heavenly city called the New Jerusalem. It has a great high wall with 12 pearly gates. The city is perfectly square and its height is equal to its length and breadth. The wall is made of jasper, and the city itself of pure gold, clear as glass. Twelve kinds of shining jewels are set in the 12 foundations of the wall, giving it a rainbow effect.[2] In this city, Jesus is called "the Lamb," because of His sacrifice for the human race. Those whose names are written in the "Lamb's Book of Life"—those who accept Jesus as their Savior from sin—can enter the city.

In the middle of the city is ShangTi's throne. From the throne flows the river of life, and on either side of the river is the tree of life.[3] God's throne is located on the majestic Mount Zion.

> Then I looked, and behold, a Lamb standing on Mount Zion, and with Him one hundred and forty-four thousand, ... [and] they sang as it were a new song before the throne.[4]

> The Lord reigns; ... He dwells between the cherubim; ... The Lord is great in Zion, and He is high above all the peoples.[5]

But wait a minute! Was there not a tree of life in the Garden of Eden, Adam and Eve's first home on earth? Yes. In addition, based on the premise that the Chinese characters convey historical fact, we believe that there was also a physical holy mountain in Eden.

The ancient symbol for *garden* ⊞ accurately pictures the four rivers arising from the center of the square garden. In other words, the Garden of Eden was an earthly miniature replica of the city of ShangTi in heaven. One ancient form of *garden* 畺 (p. 37) depicts God Ψ, with arms upraised, in the very center of the garden. The source of the rivers was the *fountain* 爪 (p. 51) of life, a unique symbol for the source of all life in ShangTi Himself.

In the second and third chapters, ShangTi was identified as the Creator of heaven, earth, and all living things on the earth. Both the venerable Chinese Border Sacrifice recitations (pp. 16, 20, 21, 27) and the ancient pictographic Chinese characters verified His creatorship. ShangTi created all things by calling them into existence (p. 27). Jesus is also identified as the Creator in the Holy Bible, where He is called the "Word," because He too spoke everything into existence:

> Before the world was created, the Word already existed; He was with God, and He was the same as God. From the very beginning the Word was with God. Through Him God made all things; not one thing in all creation was made without Him. The Word was the source of life, and this life brought light to mankind. ...
>
> The Word was in the world, and though God made the world through Him, yet the world did not recognize Him. He came to His own country, but His own people did not receive Him. Some, however, did receive Him and believed in Him; so He gave them the right to become God's children.[6]

Note that, through the "Word" (Jesus), God made all things. Jesus, the Son, was the agent of ShangTi in His creative work.

The Spirit was also an agent in creation. The three persons of the Godhead worked as one in creating our world. From the Chinese pictograms, we might be inclined to give Jesus the name of *"Shen"* 示申 , 示📿 , 示📿 (神), for this name reveals the very creative work of God in forming Adam (and Eve) with His own hands (pp. 31-32, 42-44).

Jesus Himself had declared, "The Father and I are one."[7] This is indeed a strange statement, and even His disciples did not immediately understand it. One disciple, Philip, asked, "Lord, show us the Father and that will be enough for us." To this Jesus replied:

> "Anyone who has seen Me has seen the Father.... Don't you believe that I am in the Father, and that the Father is in Me? The words I say to you are not just My own. Rather, it is the Father, living in Me, who is doing His work."[8]

This explains how the *Father* ⚘ (父) is the Creator through the agency of the Son, Shen. So the symbol ⚘ (p. 37) is thereby explained, where the *Father* ⚘ appears to be creating Adam, the *adult male* • . How truly the Chinese writing and the Hebrew Scriptures agree!

The Spirit, as just mentioned, was also an agent in creation, and this activity, too, is explicitly seen in the character for *Spirit* 靈 (p. 61-62). Here the three *persons* ᴗᴗᴗ of the Godhead (the Father, Son, and Holy Spirit) are depicted. The *work* I of creation is portrayed by the Trinity (⌐ + ⊤ + ⌐) cooperating as a *worker of magic* 工工 (p. 62).

Therefore, we can say that although ShangTi, Shen, and the Spirit are three separate persons, yet their purposes are one and their work is one. We believe that the Chinese Trinity is exactly the same as the Hebrew Godhead: the all-powerful Creator, Sustainer, and Savior of the earth; the ruler of the entire universe.

Is it any accident that when Jesus, the Son, gave His life as the Lamb 羔 of God in sacrifice for humanity's sins, that He was nailed to a cross, a *tree* 木 ? This ugly *tree* 木 of suffering has become the "tree of life" and immortality for all. In God's beautiful new city, there is no tree of the knowledge of good and evil, which formerly stood next to the tree of life in the center of the earthly garden. There will be no temptation in the new Garden of Eden, the holy city, for Satan (Lucifer, the devil, the old serpent) will have been forever destroyed.

Jesus has promised to return to our earth again. At that time, the earth will be destroyed by His glorious presence. Rebellious humanity has departed far from righteousness and followed the devil's example instead. The result has been war, bloodshed, crime, unfaithfulness, and misery. The devil has had his opportunity to demonstrate his kind of dominion and government on the earth. And now, once more, ShangTi will end the reign of sin on earth, as He did by the war in heaven (see pp. 67-68).

The second coming of Jesus will result in the end of the world. How can one be saved from the destruction and death that will sweep over the entire earth on that day? The only safe

hiding *place* 𝖻𝖻 (o)[9] (匧) will be in God's care. 匚 (o)[10]
(匚) means *to conceal, hide.* The three *persons* 𝖻𝖻 are
identified as the Trinity, the Godhead. This safe *place* 𝖻𝖻 of
hiding 匚 is only with God. The end of all things is fast approaching.

a place

While Jesus was on earth, His disciples came to Him with
the question, "What will be the sign of Your coming, and of the
end of the age?"[11] So He gave them a list of events to look for:

conceal,
hide

- False Christs and false prophets will deceive
  many.
- Wars and rumors of wars; nation rising against
  nation.
- Famines, pestilences, and earthquakes in various
  places.
- Persecution of righteous people.
- Lawlessness will increase.
- Life will go on as usual, most people unaware of
  approaching doom because of unbelief in God.
- The good news of salvation through Jesus Christ
  will be brought to every nation, and then the end
  will come.[12]

No one need be ignorant of what is coming upon the earth.
The Bible is full of warnings. But we are told that few will believe Jesus is really coming again—soon.

> You must understand that in the last days some
> people ... will make fun of you and will ask, "He
> promised to come, didn't He? Where is He? Our
> fathers have already died, but everything is still the
> same as it was since the creation of the world!"...
> But the heavens and the earth that now exist are
> being preserved by the same command of God,

in order to be destroyed by fire. They are being kept for the day when godless people will be judged and destroyed.[13]

Those faithful to God will be saved from this destruction, taken away from the earth before it is destroyed. They will be *delivered* 匡 (O)[14] (匡). By whom? The bronzeware writing of the character 匡 (B)[15] leaves no doubt that it is the *Lamb* 羊 (羊) who is the *deliverer* and will *hide* 匚 His people in that day. It will happen like this:

deliver

> The Lord Himself will come down from heaven. Those who have died believing in Christ [Jesus] will rise to life first; then we who are living at that time will be gathered up along with them in the clouds to meet the Lord in the air. And so we will always be with the Lord.[16]

Here is the answer to the question concerning death that Confucius avoided answering (p. 19). It was evidently a mystery he did not understand. However, there is a promised resurrection of all the faithful dead of all ages. Righteous people will live again (p. 98)! We can know that God, the wise judge, will deal justly.

Some will be fortunate in not having to taste death at all—"we who are living at that time." These faithful ones will be taken directly to heaven on that day when Jesus returns. And what of the earth?

> On that Day the heavens will disappear with a shrill noise, the heavenly bodies will burn up and be destroyed, and the earth with everything in it will vanish.[17]

But ShangTi has promised a new earth after the destruction of the present one, with the eradication of sin and sinners. The disciple John, when an old man, related what he saw in a heavenly vision:

> Then I saw a new heaven and a new earth. The first heaven and the first earth disappeared, and the sea vanished. And I saw the Holy City, the new Jerusalem, coming down out of heaven from God, prepared and ready, like a bride dressed to meet her husband. I heard a loud voice speaking from the throne: "Now God's home is with mankind! He will live with them, and they shall be His people. God Himself will be with them, and He will be their God. He will wipe away all tears from their eyes. There will be no more death, no more grief or crying or pain. The old things have disappeared."[18]

God will make His dwelling place with people on the "new earth" which will then become the capital of the entire universe. His *imperial domain* 㘴 (p. 54), His throne, will be in their midst. How appropriate that again the miniature of God's beautiful city, the *garden* ⊞ of Eden, appears in this character! Rising above all in this beautiful celestial garden in the new Jerusalem is God's lofty throne on Mount Zion. The disciple John related more of his vision:

> The angel also showed me the river of the water of life, sparkling like crystal, and coming from the throne of God and of the Lamb and flowing down the middle of the city's street. On each side of the river is the tree of life, which bears fruit twelve times a year, once each month....

The throne of God and of the Lamb will be in the city, and His servants will worship Him. They will see his face.... There shall be no more night ... because the Lord God will be their light, and they will rule as kings forever and ever.[19]

The *imperial domain* 田 depicts God's *garden* ⊞ paradise and the great *Being* ⼂ , God Himself.

This earth and its human inhabitants have, since creation, been the object of ShangTi's greatest love and concern. Very soon, the lengthy controversy between ShangTi and the devil will be over. The war has already been decided. We must be on the right side—the winning side! God gives the invitation to all:

Come, whoever is thirsty; accept the water of life as a gift, whoever wants it.[20]

There will be no more *barrier* 𝄃𝄃 at the garden *gate* ⼓ ⼓. All who have the Lamb's gift of *righteousness* 羕 may freely come and go into the new Garden of Eden. No one will be excluded from the *tree* 朩 of life. Everyone may eat the fruit that gives everlasting life. Best of all, we can all *meet* 覺 face-to-face (pp. 57, 80) with ShangTi, as did Adam and Eve in the beginning.

Blessed are those who do His commandments, that they may have the right to the tree of life, and may enter through the gates into the city.[21]

Furthermore, God promises,

"To those who win the victory I will give the right to

eat the fruit of the tree of life that grows in the Garden of God."[22]

Let the ancient Chinese characters speak truth to you. These must have been preserved in the earth for more than 4,000 years, until our very day, to convince us that ShangTi still lives. The great Sovereign of heaven, Creator of the earth, loves and has a vital interest in each individual.

ShangTi

> For I am certain that nothing can separate us from His love: neither death nor life, neither angels nor other heavenly rulers or powers, neither the present nor the future, neither the world above nor the world below—there is nothing in all creation that will ever be able to separate us from the love of God which is ours through Christ Jesus our Lord.[23]

Imperial Sacrifice

Now we can fully appreciate the various oracle bone renderings of Ti (ShangTi). In this ancient script, we have found the original *Ruler(Ti)* 帝 (帝) of heaven and earth represented as the Trinity, three *persons* ▷ + ▽ + ◁ (compare ϝ , p. 60; 禜 , pp. 61-62). He was also Creator, represented by the "speaking" aspect of the *mouths* (see p. 30).

A "shorthand form" of *Ti*, the *Ruler*, is 帝 (o).[24] In this figure, two *God* symbols ⊢ + ⊣ replace the *person* radicals ▷ + ◁ . The character *Imperial Sacrifice (Border Sacrifice)* 禘 (o)[25] (禘) uses this form, where the *hands* 廾 of the two worshipers praise Ti (ShangTi) 帝 .

morally pure, central focus, a plan

One more very meaningful character remains for our contemplation. Additional forms and meanings of 方 (方 , p. 54) reveal the Trinity, ⊢ + ⊤ + ⊣ in 方 (o)[26] (方) and especially characterize Jesus, the Son, in its definitions: *morally pure, central focus, a plan.* If we superimpose this figure on the *tree* 朩 , a new form of *ShangTi* 禾(O)[27] appears. When Jesus, morally pure, was nailed to the cross, He became a central focus and completed God's rescue plan for humanity. The cross became the tree of llife for each of us: [Christ] who Himself bore our sins in His own body on the tree."[28]

And so our Confucian riddles are completely solved! There is just one more fact. This great, loving ShangTi is still searching, yearning, and pleading for lost people everywhere to return to Him:

> "Turn to Me now and be saved,
>   people all over the world!
> I am the only God there is.
> My promise is true,
>   and it will not be changed.
> I solemnly promise by all that I am."[29]

A New Look
at an Old Language

When Hsu Shen compiled his time-honored *Shuo Wen* in 86 B.C., he not only set forth to the best of his ability the authentic character forms but also made a first meager attempt to explain the derivation of many pictographic and ideographic characters from familiar objects of his day. The *Shuo Wen* has been the basis for analysis of Chinese characters since that time, with many more recent scholars adding their own ideas of interpretation as the years passed. But at least 2,000 years had elapsed in Hsu Shen's day since the invention of the writing, and today the venerable characters are more than 4,000 years old. Might there have been another, more methodical system used by the ancient Chinese as the basis upon which to build their language than everyday objects?

Ancient Egyptian scribes also had their own intricate pictographic writing, called hieroglyphs, meaning "sacred writing." Built right into their script were their peculiar religious concepts. We believe that the Chinese, too, may have created a hieroglyphic writing to preserve their sacred tenets, as our book has demonstrated. In other words, instead of a hit-or-miss calligraphy depicting only objects about them in their everyday life (which may have been very different from the world 2,000 or 4,000 years later), it is possible that the Chinese of antiquity had a real plan for their writing. This system might have been based upon their knowledge of the God, ShangTi, whom they worshiped at that time, and the relationship of God to the first human couple: namely, a record of the beginnings of human history and the interplay between God and people.

A brief, and of course incomplete, comparison between the existing method of character analysis and our "hieroglyphic" concept will be given to illustrate the plausibility of a systematic, graphic language that depicts actual sacred, historical narratives and facts.

First of all, we believe that God has, in the past, been little appreciated in the ancients' multiple artistic configurations depicting Him. These are important to recognize:

1. Pictograms ("stick figures") of God, always with *arms* upraised in blessing, for example: Ψ (Ψ, Ψ, p.29; ⊞, p. 37; 圀, p. 51; ⅋, p. 57); ⊢ (⟁, p. 37; ⧄, p. 41; 卬, p. 79); ⊩ (𩵋, p. 85); ⊓ (𣲷, p. 55; 卬, p. 55); Ⅹ (𤣩, p. 45; ⅄, p. 56); and ⅄ (⊞, p. 37; 田ᐣ, p. 54; 𤣩, p. 61).

2. Representations of God as a great *person, being,* for example: ⼁ (⧗, p. 44; 𢀪, p. 42; 田, p. 128); ⫝ (⧄, p. 70); ◌ (◌, p. 41); ⼌ (⧄, p. 66). Remember also

134

that Adam and Eve were made in God's image, to look like Him. For example: ⟩ (⟨⟩ , p. 32; ⟨⟩ , p. 32; ⟨⟩ , p. 55; ⟨⟩ , p. 56; ⟨⟩ , p. 79); ⟨⟩ (⟨⟩ , p. 32; ⟨⟩ , p. 36).

3. A symbol of *God's presence* ⟨⟩ , representing the three members of the Godhead, the Trinity, may be found in various arrangements: ⟨⟩ (⟨⟩, p.62); ⟨⟩ (⟨⟩ , p. 62); ⟨⟩ (⟨⟩ , p. 91); ⟨⟩ (⟨⟩ , p. 117).

4. Use of the *God* radicals ⟨⟩ , ⟨⟩ , the most primitive being ⊤ or ⊤̄ (⟨⟩, p. 48; ⟨⟩ , p. 49; ⟨⟩ , p. 54; ⟨⟩ , p. 69).

5. Recognition of God's creative *hand(s)* ⟨⟩ (⟨⟩ , p. 29; ⟨⟩ , p. 42); ⟨⟩ (⟨⟩ , p. 32); ⟨⟩ (⟨⟩ , p. 42; ⟨⟩ , p. 44), etc.

6. Identification of God's earthly meeting place with Adam and Eve—a holy *mountain*, for example: ⟨⟩ (⟨⟩ , p. 55); ⟨⟩ (⟨⟩ , p. 56); ⟨⟩ (⟨⟩, p.62); ⟨⟩ (⟨⟩, p. 79).

Second, we must recognize the first human couple, often conjoined (married), as more than just "two ordinary persons." In their sinless state they were sometimes decorated with a *flame of fire* • , symbolizing their reflection of God's glory. For example: ⟨⟩ (⟨⟩ , p. 44; ⟨⟩ , p. 45; ⟨⟩ , p. 55; ⟨⟩ , p. 68). They may be identified as *persons, mouths*, for example: ⟨⟩ (⟨⟩, p. 45); ⟨⟩ (⟨⟩, p.46); ⟨⟩ (⟨⟩, p. 46); ⟨⟩ (⟨⟩ , p. 46); ⟨⟩ (⟨⟩, p. 50); ⟨⟩ (⟨⟩ , p. 85; ⟨⟩ , p. 85; ⟨⟩, p. 85; ⟨⟩, p. 85). In many characters they are depicted as bowing figures: ⟨⟩ (⟨⟩, p. 55; ⟨⟩ , p. 55; ⟨⟩, p. 65; ⟨⟩ , p. 66; ⟨⟩ , p. 77). Another ancient calligrapher's trick is to portray Eve emerging from Adam, as in ⟨⟩ (⟨⟩ p. 51;

～ , p. 75); ٯ , p. 42; ٯ , p. 44; ⊞ǂ , p. 53. Conjoined hands or a pair of worshiping hands also designate the first pair, for example: ۴ (ㄨㄨ , p. 60; ㄫ , p. 87; ㄆ , p. 130); ✕ (ㄝ, p. 85; ㄇㄫ, p. 86).

Third, we may find in the characters various features of the Garden of Eden home of the first couple: the *garden* ⊞ , ⊞, ⊕ , ⊞, (pp. 51, 52, 53, 54, 56, 68, 77); the holy *mountain* (as above); a *fountain* (ㄤ , p. 51; ㄤ , p. 63); a holy *place* (ㄈㄒ , p. 56; ㄩ, p. 126); a *river* ⧵⧵ (pp. 51, 56, 85, 117); two special *trees* ㄨㄨ (pp. 50, 54, 55, 60, 69, 72, 73, 75); or the garden *gate* ▷◁ , ۴۴ , ㄗㄟ (pp. 82, 86).

It becomes obvious why so many artistic variations for each of these depicted objects were necessary, as a single theme might be used repeatedly to express a great spectrum of appropriate meanings.

As the following illustrative samples are given to demonstrate the two theories of analysis (the *Shuo Wen* and our "hieroglyphic" method), one can readily observe that the *Shuo Wen* actually contains little analysis, being in reality more of a dictionary. Hsu Shen had no access to either the bronzeware or oracle bone writings. His recorded characters are all in the seal writing. Consequently, he was disadvantaged in not being able to see the earliest, more pictographic, forms. Therefore his comments prove disappointing.

For our comparison, we will discuss a number of characters describing the narrative of the two special trees in the Garden of Eden. This story can be arranged nicely in chronological sequence. Pagination of our in-depth analyses, which may be reviewed in the book's main text, will be cited in parentheses. Alternate interpretations taken directly from the *Shuo Wen* will be found in quotation marks. Comparison of the two methods will give one the opportunity to decide if the ancient Chinese had a unique method of recording sacred, historical data.

Both we and Hsu Shen believe that the character 示申 (神 , p. 31) refers to God, the Creator. Hsu Shen explains the meaning of this character with the phrase, "The God of Heaven [天神] leads out all creation."[1] He analyzes the character as being phonetic, composed of 示 and 申 , since the right-hand symbol, 申 , has the same sound, "shen," as the entire character. He states that 示 , which we identify as the God radical (p. 31), indicates "a revelation, auspicious or unlucky, from heaven. The two 二 horizontal lines [in 上] are the old form of 上 , (meaning *supreme, above*); and the 小 represents sun, moon and stars, or signs in heaven which reveal transcendent things to men."[2] Hsu Shen does not explain the right-hand figure 申 we interpret as God creating *man* 丨 by His *hands* 𦥑 (p. 31).

As anyone acquainted with Chinese characters will quickly recognize, we have given "ideographic" interpretation to many characters commonly classified as "phonetic." Hsu Shen probably originated this classification when he noted the phonetic similarity between a constituent radical and the character as a whole. Since he was unable to make ideographic sense from the character, he must have concluded that this hodge-podge of radicals was drawn together only because of similarity in sound.

We would like to emphasize once more, however, that there were remarkable phonetic associations in the spoken language between words long before writing was invented. We have pointed out in the text (pp. 33, 51, 88) only a few of many recognized phonetic associations.

We will use seven characters, all containing the common symbol *tree* 木 or *trees* 林林 to relate the dramatic story of how sin entered our world. These characters are *to restrict, prevent* 木 (杜); *to travel* 木呂 (枢); *to stop, rest* 休 (休); *to covet, desire* 林 (婪); *sorrow* 林 , 楚 (楚); *barrier, fence* 閒 (閑); and *trouble, worry* 困 (困).

The warning of *restriction* 木 (杜) not to eat from the forbidden *tree* 木 was given to Adam (p. 69), the man of *dust* 土 . According to Hsu Shen, the character merely indicates a "sweet crab apple"[4] and the *dust* 土 (土) radical is only phonetic.

Adam and Eve, the *couple* 呂 (p. 44), probably *traveled* 木呂 (枢) daily to the *tree* 木 to partake of the fruit giving immortality. Quoting Hsu Shen, " 枢 means the lintel of a door; 呂 is the phonetic."[5]

The character *to stop, rest* 休 (休) can represent Eve, the *person* 亻 who *stopped* alone, at the forbidden *tree* 木 (p. 70). Hsu Shen merely says the word means "to stop and rest," whereas a later scholar warns "one must not stop under a tall tree and think."[6] This particular tree mentioned, 喬 , is not a fruit tree, but one used for making furniture.

Hsu Shen states regarding *desire, covet* 㜲 (婪) that it means "to covet or be greedy and is composed of 林 and 女 , being phonetic with 林 ."[7] We believe the *woman* 𠨧 (女) represents Eve who was the first person to *covet* anything. She *desired* the fruit from the forbidden *tree* 木 , which stood next to the *tree* 木 of life (p.73).

Sorrow 楚 (楚 , p. 78) Hsu Shen explains simply as "a shrub or kind of bramble and is composed of 林 and 疋 , being phonetic with 疋 ."[8] In the ancient form 楚 , we can clearly see a *person* ○ *stopped* 𠤎 (止) and eating (with the *mouth* ○). A second ancient form, 楚 , actually depicts Eve picking fruit 𠤎 from the forbidden *tree* 木 . This act of disobedience brought *sorrow* to all humanity.

It was necessary for God to set up a *barrier* 閑 (閑) at the *gate* 門 from which the disobedient couple had been expelled. They could no longer eat of the *tree* 木 of life or have immortality (p. 82). Hsu Shen merely defines this character as a "fence"[9] and does not try to give a reason for these radicals being brought together.

To worry 困 (p. 79), deciphered by Hsu Shen, becomes "an old thatched house"[10]—which is a far cry from the real reason for the first couple's worry. A second oracle bone rendition of this character 困 gives the reason for the trouble: it was because Eve *stopped* 𠤎 at the *tree* 木 (abbreviated). Of course it was the forbidden *tree* 木 in the garden *enclosure* ☐ that had given the first couple cause for worry, trouble, and difficulty.

This short calligraphic series demonstrates how easy it is to follow a whole story by various pictographic and ideographic characters.

The solution to the sin problem brought about by eating of the forbidden *tree* 木 is found in the *sheep* 𡴎 (羊) and *bull* 牛 (牛) sacrifices, which represented the vicarious death of the Savior, God's Son, one member of the Godhead. In four characters featuring the *sheep* 𡴎 , we see this plan of salvation explained: *sacrificial animals* 犧 (犧); *righteous* 義 (義); *beautiful* 美 (美); and *to deliver* 匡 (匡).

For 犧 , Hsu Shen records "sacrificial animals for the temple, composed of 羊 and 牛 , and being phonetic with 義 ."[11] We agree that this character names the *sacrificial animals,* but we believe these sacrifices were initiated at the Garden of Eden and were again symbolic and prophetic of the sacrifice of God's only Son, Jesus. *Bull* 牛 and *sheep* 𡴎 sacrifices were also used by the Hebrews in their sacrifices to the God of Heaven, even as the Chinese did in their Border Sacrifices to ShangTi (p. 87).

Righteous 義 , Hsu Shen explains as "righteousness in my appearance, being composed of *I, me, my* 我 and *sheep* 羊 ."[12] In our analysis, we indicate more fully the significance of this beautiful character. *I* 我 am made *righteous* 義 by the death of the *Lamb* 𡴎 of God (p. 84).

140

The character *beautiful* 美 is explained by Hsu Shen as "sweet, delicious, being composed of 羊 and 大 ." More interestingly he says that "of the six livestock animals used for food, the sheep is the most important."[13] We believe the sheep was the most important animal because of its symbolic representation of God's Son, the *Lamb* of God, whose sacrificial death would make us *beautiful* in God's eyes. Therefore, we analyze 美 as a *sheep* 羊 covering a *noble man* 大 , originally Adam. God would see only His sinless Son when looking upon the sinner thus covered by the Lamb (p. 84).

Lastly, we find the *sheep* 羊 once more featured in 匯 (匡), meaning appropriately *to deliver*, for it is the *Lamb* 羊 of God only who can *deliver* all from sin (p. 127). This character's analysis of a "rice container,"[14] in the *Shuo Wen*, again demonstrates the disadvantage of Hsu Shen in not having the bronzeware character to examine.

We have presented only a brief comparison of the two methods of analysis. It will be obvious to the reader that Hsu Shen, for the most part, defined the meaning of characters and did very little interpretation. He certainly did not attempt to discover why the characters were composed of specific radicals, as we have done. In his time, besides having no access to the most ancient characters, he knew nothing of the historical records of humanity's origin, namely the Hebrew writings, as contained in the Bible. We are now fortunate to be able to examine these for similarities with the ancient Chinese ideographic characters.

Perhaps the above gives some insight into the logical system of "hieroglyphic," or "hierographic," writing, built upon the ancients' knowledge of their world and the loving relationship between earth's first people and their Creator God, ShangTi. How wonderful that we, 4,000 years later, can glimpse this primeval earth through the medium of well-stored pictures and ideas!

Appendix

Synchronizing Chinese and Biblical History

How did the ancient Chinese acquire the same historical facts regarding creation, the temptation and fall of the first human couple, and a similar sacrificial worship system as the Hebrew people? How could two geographically separated peoples have extensive identical data if this information is based upon mere legends?

To answer these questions, we need to compare the earliest Chinese dynastic records with the earth chronology recorded in the Bible. Contained within the first eleven chapters of Genesis (the first book of the Bible) are answers to the enigma. We will find that the early Chinese were contemporaries and descendants of the biblical man named Noah. In Genesis chapters 5 and 10 are detailed genealogies of earth's first inhabitants from which accurate chronological data can be accrued. We examine this record, beginning with chapter 5:

> This is the book of the genealogy of Adam. In the day that God created man, He made him in the

likeness of God. He created them male and female, and blessed them and called them Mankind in the day they were created. And Adam lived one hundred and thirty years, and begot a son in his own likeness, after his image, and named him Seth. After he begot Seth, the days of Adam were eight hundred years; and he begot sons and daughters. So all the days that Adam lived were nine hundred and thirty years; and he died.

Seth lived one hundred and five years, and begot Enosh. After he begot Enosh, Seth lived eight hundred and seven years, and begot sons and daughters. So all the days of Seth were nine hundred and twelve years; and he died.

Enosh lived ninety years, and begot Cainan. After he begot Cainan, Enosh lived eight hundred and fifteen years, and begot sons and daughters. So all the days of Enosh were nine hundred and five years; and he died.[1]

For us, living on the verge of the 21st century A.D., the above reads like a fairy tale. It would seem highly improbable that Adam lived 930 years, Seth 912 years, and Enosh 905 years. This certainly doesn't sound like today's life expectancy—and it isn't. Evidently, their beautiful earth was completely free of any life-shortening contamination. Why should not early humans have lived nearly 1,000 years? As we examine the rest of the genealogies of Genesis 5, we learn that the life spans of the first 10 generations of men averaged 912 years. But something happened during the 10th generation.

Then the Lord saw that the wickedness of man was great in the earth, and that every intent of the thoughts of his heart was only evil continually. And the Lord was sorry that He had made man on the earth, and He was grieved in His heart. So the Lord said, "I will destroy man whom I have created from the face of the earth, both man and beast, creeping thing and birds of the air, for I am sorry that I have made them." But Noah found grace in the eyes of the Lord.... Noah was a just man, perfect in his generations. Noah walked with God.[2]

Yet God waited another 120 years after making His decision, while Noah and his three sons built a great ship and preached righteousness to earth's evil inhabitants. However, these godly men met only derision from the world's wicked inhabitants. Finally, God sent a mighty worldwide flood to destroy all of earth's peoples, except for this man's family of eight persons (Noah, his wife, their sons, and their wives). Pairs of all kinds of animals entered the ark prior to the flood and were likewise borne to safety through the deluge. From the accurate genealogical chronology of Adam's descendants recorded in the Bible, we know that the great flood took place 1656 years after creation.

Then, it was only 101 years after the flood (calculated from the genealogical data of Genesis, chapter 11) when another event of great importance took place. In the fifth generation after Noah, we read of this incident:

To Eber [son of Salah, son of Arphaxad, son of Shem, son of Noah] were born two sons: the name of one was Peleg, for in his days the earth was divided.[3]

At the time of the birth of this child, just 101 years after the flood, the Bible tells us "the earth was divided." If we read on, we learn the reason:

> Now the whole earth had one language and one speech. ... And they [men on the plain of Shinar] said, "Come, let us build ourselves a city, and a tower whose top is in the heavens; let us make a name for ourselves, lest we be scattered abroad over the face of the whole earth."

> But the Lord came down to see the city and the tower which the sons of men had built. And the Lord said, "Indeed the people are one and they all have one language, and this is what they begin to do; now nothing that they propose to do will be withheld from them. Come, let Us go down and there confuse their language, that they may not understand one another's speech." So the Lord scattered them abroad from there over the face of all the earth, and they ceased building the city. Therefore its name is called Babel, because there the Lord confused the language of all the earth; and from there the Lord scattered them abroad over the face of all the earth.[4]

At this very time, the varied languages of earth originated, including the Chinese language. In what year did this event take place? Our calendar reckonings used today are based upon the year of Christ Jesus' birth. The years before His birth are called "B.C." (before Christ), and the years after His birth, "A.D." (Latin, *anno Domini*, meaning "in the year of the Lord"). We have already stated that the flood took place 1656 years after creation. But how many years B.C. was this?

Many historical facts and periods of various kings' reigns are recorded in the Bible. James Ussher (1581-1656), an Irish archbishop of Armagh, did a monumental study, gathering time-related biblical information and correlating this with known historically dated records. He concluded that the flood took place about 2348 B.C,[5] which would place the Tower of Babel incident, with the scattering of peoples over the earth, at about 2247 B.C. Note that the first dynasty [Hsia] in China is recorded as beginning in 2205 B.C.[6] If Ussher's figures are close to correct in dating the dispersion incident at about 2247 B.C., this gives approximately 40 years for a migration of the great Chinese family from the region of the Tower of Babel in Mesopotamia to resettlement in China. How closely these dates correspond!

But that is not all! Before the first dynasty in 2205 B.C., the Chinese record a mysterious "Legendary Period of Five Rulers." It was during this period that Chinese history records in the *Shu Ching [Book of History]*, compiled by Confucius, that a ruler, Shun by name (c. 2230 B.C.), "sacrificed to ShangTi."[7] How does this fit into the puzzle?

There were just five generations between the flood and the Tower of Babel. It was the duty and privilege of the successive patriarchs of the family (e.g., Noah, Shem, Arphaxad, Salah, Eber) to offer sheep and bullock sacrifices to God in anticipation of the sacrifice of God's Son, Jesus, who would one day give His sinless life for sinful humanity. Could not the Chinese "five rulers" have been five patriarchs in the Chinese family of

Noah's descendants and the ruler Shun been one of these patriarchs? This would fit exactly with both the Chinese records and information cited from the Hebrew Scriptures.

> These were the families of the sons of Noah, according to their generations, in their nations; and from these the nations were divided on the earth after the flood.[8]

Since all peoples of earth are descended from Noah or his sons, the early Chinese ancestors could have been contemporaries of Noah (who lived 350 years after the flood). Therefore, information could have been passed to them by word-of-mouth, even by Noah himself. He, in turn, obtained his historical data from his father, Lamech, who was 56 years old when Adam died. Thus, all the details of creation and life before the flood could have been passed to the Chinese from Adam with only two intermediaries, Lamech and Noah. No wonder the Chinese ideographic characters, in which these historical narratives are stored, agree completely with the stories later recorded in Genesis by Moses (a descendant of Eber, father of Peleg and patriarch of the Hebrews). The source of historical authenticity was the same for both the ancient Chinese and Moses.

References

1: The Riddle

1. James Legge, *The Chinese Classics* (vol. iii), *The Shoo King: Canon of Shun* (Taipei: Southern Materials Center Inc.,1983), pp. 33-34.
2. James Legge, *The Notions of the Chinese Concerning God and Spirits* (Hong Kong: Hong Kong Register Office, 1852), pp. 24-25.
3. *Ibid.*, p. 30.
4. *Ibid.*, p. 31.

2: Who Is ShangTi?

1. James Legge, *The Notions of the Chinese Concerning God and Spirits* (Hong Kong: Hong Kong Register Office, 1852), p. 28.
2. *Ibid.*, p. 29.
3. *Ibid.*, p. 29.
4. *Ibid.*, p. 30.
5. *Ibid.*, pp. 50-51.
6. Lung Ch'uan Kwei T'ai Lang, *Shih Chi Hui Chu K'ao Cheng* (Taipei: Han Ching Wen Hua Enterprise Co. Ltd., 1983), p. 496.
7. Hsin Cheng Yu, *Ancient Chinese History* (Taipei: Taiwan Commercial Press, 1963), p. 6.

8. Bradley Smith and Wan-go Weng, *China, a History in Art* (New York: Doubleday, 1972), p. 33.
9. G. D. Wilder and J. H. Ingram, *Analysis of Chinese Characters* (Taipei: Chin Wen Publ. Co., 1964), pp. iv-vi.
10. Genesis 1:1-2, 9-10, 16, 27-28 NKJV.

3: Chinese Concepts of Earth's Human Beginnings

1. James Legge, *The Notions of the Chinese Concerning God and Spirits* (Hong Kong: Hong Kong Register Office, 1852), p. 29.
2. Psalm 33:6, 9 TEV.
3. Genesis 1:24 NKJV.
4. Hung Pei Chiang, *Chih Ku Lu Chuan Wen* (Taipei: Lo Tien Publ. Co., 1974), vol. ii, p. 1169.
5. *Ibid.*, p. 1341.
6. *Ibid.*, p. 1251.
7. Ma Wei Ching, *Wei Ching Chia Ku Wen Yuan* (Yunlin: Ma Fu Distributor, 1971), p. 727. See also Hung Pei Chiang, *Ching Wen P'ien Ching Wen* (Taipei: Kung I Publ. Co., 1974), pp. 384-385.
8. Ma Wei Ching, p. 183.
9. Lin Chih Ch'ing, *Ting Cheng Liu Shu T'ung* (Shanghai: Kuang-I Publ. Co., 1936), section 1, part ii, p. 12.
10. Hung Pei Chiang, *Chih Ku Lu Chuan Wen*, vol. i, p. 351.
11. *Ibid.*, vol. ii, p. 949.
12. Genesis 2:7 KJV.
13. Lin Chih Ch'ing, section 1, part viii, p. 35.
14. Ma Wei Ching, p. 472.
15. Lin Chih Ch'ing, section 1, part i, p. 34.
16. Ma Wei Ching, p. 385.
17. Hung Pei Chiang, *Ching Wen P'ien Ching Wen*, p. 495.
18. *Ibid.*, p. 473.
19. *Ibid.*, p. 393.
20. Lin Chih Ch'ing, section 1, part viii, p. 6.
21. Genesis 1:26 TEV.
22. Psalm 84:11 KJV.

23. Deuteronomy 4:24 KJV.
24. Hung Pei Chiang, *Chih Ku Lu Chuan Wen*, vol. ii, p. 1341.
25. Psalm 104:1-2 NKJV.
26. Hung Pei Chiang, *Chih Ku Lu Chuan Wen*, vol. ii, p. 1302.
27. Genesis 1:26 TEV.
28. Lung Ch'uan Kwei T'ai Lang, *Shih Chi Hui Chu K'ao Cheng* (Taipei: Han Ching Wen Hua Enterprise Co. Ltd., 1983), p. 497.
29. Hung Pei Chiang, *Chih Ku Lu Chuan Wen*, vol. ii, p. 1010.
30. Lin Chih Ch'ing, section 1, part iii, p. 1.
31. Hung Pei Chiang, *Ching Wen P'ien Ching Wen*, p. 593.
32. Genesis 2:25 NIV.
33. Hung Pei Chiang, *Chih Ku Lu Chuan Wen*, vol. ii, p. 1162.
34. Psalm 8:5 NRSV.
35. Chou Fa Kao, et al., *Ching Wen Ku Lin* (Hong Kong: Chinese University, 1975), p. 5526.
36. Hung Pei Chiang, *Chih Ku Lu Chuan Wen*, vol. i, p. 49.
37. Legge, p. 29.
38. Hung Pei Chiang, *Chih Ku Lu Chuan Wen*, vol. i, p. 50.
39. Hung Pei Chiang, *Ching Wen P'ien Ching Wen*, p. 212.
40. Ma Wei Ching, p. 106.
41. Hung Pei Chiang, *Chih Ku Lu Chuan Wen*, vol. ii, p. 1158.
42. Legge, p. 29.
43. Isaiah 64:8 NIV.
44. Genesis 2:7 KJV.
45. Ma Wei Ching, p. 1308.
46. Lin Chih Ch'ing, section 1, part vii, p. 17.
47. Ma Wei Ching, p. 22.
48. *Ibid.*, p. 498.
49. Hung Pei Chiang, *Ching Wen P'ien Ching Wen*, p. 541.
50. *Ibid.*, p. 545.
51. Genesis 2:19-20 TEV.

52. Genesis 2:18 TEV.
53. Chou Fa Kao, p. 6776.
54. Ma Wei Ching, p. 549.
55. Hung Pei Chiang, *Ching Wen P'ien Ching Wen*, p. 645.
56. *Ibid.*, p. 544.
57. Job 33:4 NKJV.

4: The Rib Story

1. Hung Pei Chiang, *Chih Ku Lu Chuan Wen* (Taipei: Lo Tien Publ. Co., 1974), vol. ii, p. 1305.
2. *Ibid.*, vol. ii, p. 1014.
3. Genesis 2:18, 21-22 TEV.
4. Ma Wei Ching, *Wei Ching Chia Ku Wen Yuan* (Yunlin: Ma Fu Distributor, 1971), p. 39.
5. *Ibid.*, p. 542.
6. *Ibid.*, p. 529.
7. Lin Chih Ch'ing, *Ting Cheng Liu Shu T'ung* (Shanghai: Kuang-I Publ. Co., 1936), section 1, part viii, p. 33 under 月豆..
8. Ma Wei Ching, p. 549.
9. *Ibid.*, p. 541, under 妾 .
10. Genesis 2:23 TEV.
11. Ma Wei Ching, p. 806.
12. Hung Pei Chiang, *Ching Wen P'ien Ching Wen* (Taipei: Kung I Publ. Co., 1974), p. 368.
13. Ma Wei Ching, p. 45.
14. Hung Pei Chiang, *Ching Wen P'ien Ching Wen*, p. 414.
15. Hung Pei Chiang, *Chih Ku Lu Chuan Wen*, vol. ii, p. 1012.
16. Genesis 2:23 NKJV.
17. Ma Wei Ching, p. 541.
18. Hung Pei Chiang, *Chih Ku Lu Chuan Wen*, vol. ii, p. 1115.
19. Genesis 1:28 RSV.
20. Lin Chih Ch'ing, section 1, part ii, p. 12.
21. *Ibid.*

22. Chou Fa Kao, et al., *Ching Wen Ku Lin* (Hong Kong: Chinese University, 1975), p. 8354.
23. Hung Pei Chiang, *Chih Ku Lu Chuan Wen,* vol. ii, p. 940.
24. *Ibid.,* p. 809.
25. Chou Fa Kao, p. 4775.
26. Ma Wei Ching, p. 1184.
27. Genesis 2:24 NIV.
28. Lin Chih Ch'ing, section 1, part i, p. 9.
29. Ma Wei Ching, p. 473.
30. Genesis 2:25 TEV.
31. Ma Wei Ching, p. 75.
32. *Ibid.*
33. Hung Pei Chiang, *Chih Ku Lu Chuan Wen,* vol. ii, p. 1173.
34. Genesis 2:1-3 NIV.
35. Ma Wei Ching, p. 1340.
36. Lin Chih Ch'ing, section 1, part viii, p. 21.
37. Ma Wei Ching, p. 1190.
38. Li Hsiao Ting, *Chia Ku Wen Tzu Chi Shih* (Thesis No. 50, Chung Yang Yen Chiu Yuan Li Shih Yan Yu Yan Chiu So, 1965), p. 447.
39. *Ibid.*
40. Ma Wei Ching, p. 1025.
41. *Ibid.,* p. 1019.

5: Secrets of a Lost Garden

1. Chou Fa Kao, et al., *Ching Wen Ku Lin* (Hong Kong: Chinese University, 1975), p. 12.
2. *Ibid.,* p. 13.
3. Genesis 3:20 NKJV.
4. Ma Wei Ching, *Wei Ching Chia Ku Wen Yuan* (Yunlin: Ma Fu Distributor, 1971), p. 783.
5. *Ibid.,* p. 1090.
6. Genesis 2:8-10 RSV.

7. Hung Pei Chiang, *Chih Ku Lu Chuan Wen* (Taipei: Lo Tien Publ. Co., 1974), vol. ii, p. 1233.
8. Lin Chih Ch'ing, *Ting Cheng Liu Shu T'ung* (Shanghai: Kuang-I Publ. Co., 1936), section 2, part iii, p. 2.
9. Ma Wei Ching, p. 57.
10. *Ibid.*, p. 1019.
11. Lin Chih Ch'ing, section 1, part iii, p. 11.
12. Psalm 36:6-9 RSV.
13. Ma Wei Ching, p. 107.
14. *Ibid.*, p. 1405.
15. Jeremiah 27:5 NIV.
16. William Morris, editor, *The American Heritage Dictionary* (Boston: Houghton Mifflin Co., 1973), p. 108.
17. Ma Wei Ching, p. 108.
18. *Ibid.*
19. *Ibid.*, p. 105.
20. Genesis 2:15 NKJV.
21. *Ibid.*, p. 589.
22. Genesis 2:9 NIV.
23. Ma Wei Ching, p. 121.
24. *Ibid.*, p. 1252.
25. Hung Pei Chiang, *Ching Wen P'ien Ching Wen* (Taipei: Kung I Publ. Co., 1974), p. 519.
26. Chou Fa Kao, p. 4235.
27. Hung Pei Chiang, *Ching Wen P'ien Ching Wen*, p. 347.
28. *Ibid.*, p. 368.
29. Ma Wei Ching, p. 898.
30. Hung Pei Chiang, *Ching Wen P'ien Ching Wen*, p. 350.
31. *Ibid.*, p. 753.
32. Ma Wei Ching, p. 117.
33. *Ibid.*, p. 116.
34. Psalm 24:3-5 RSV.
35. Hung Pei Chiang, *Ching Wen P'ien Ching Wen*, p. 222.
36. Hung Pei Chiang, *Chih Ku Lu Chuan Wen*, vol. ii, p. 1211.

6: More on the Nature of ShangTi

1. Chou Fa Kao, et al., *Ching Wen Ku Lin* (Hong Kong: Chinese University, 1975), p. 5699.
2. Ma Wei Ching, *Wei Ching Chia Ku Wen Yuan* (Yunlin: Ma Fu Distributor, 1971), p. 81.
3. Chou Fa Kao, p. 5699.
4. Ma Wei Ching, p. 81.
5. *Ibid.*, p. 70.
6. *Ibid.*, p. 70.
7. *Ibid.*, p. 70.
8. *Ibid.*, p. 72.
9. Hung Pei Chiang, *Chih Ku Lu Chuan Wen* (Taipei: Lo Tien Publ. Co., 1974), vol. ii, p. 878.
10. *Ibid.*, p. 853.
11. *Ibid.*, p. 1044.
12. *Ibid.*, p. 916.
13. *Ibid.*, p. 803.
14. Genesis 1:1-2 KJV.
15. Psalm 104:29-30 NIV.
16. Genesis 2:7 TEV.
17. Lin Chih Ch'ing, *Ting Cheng Liu Shu T'ung* (Shanghai: Kuang-I Publ. Co., 1936), section 1, part iv, p. 24.
18. *Ibid.*, section 1, part i, p. 46.
19. Hung Pei Chiang, *Ching Wen P'ien Ching Wen* (Taipei: Kung I Publ. Co., 1974), p. 280.
20. Ma Wei Ching, p. 1297.
21. Chou Fa Kao, p. 290.
22. Hung Pei Chiang, *Ching Wen P'ien Ching Wen*, p. 54.
23. Ma Wei Ching, p. 1308.
24. Hung Pei Chiang, *Chih Ku Lu Chuan Wen*, vol. ii, p. 841.
25. Ma Wei Ching, p. 1197.
26. Hung Pei Chiang, *Ching Wen P'ien Ching Wen*, p. 437.
27. Lin Chih Ch'ing, section 1, part iii, p. 30.

7: Invader in the Garden

1. Chou Fa Kao, et al., *Ching Wen Ku Lin* (Hong Kong: Chinese University, 1975), p. 86.
2. Ma Wei Ching, *Wei Ching Chia Ku Wen Yuan* (Yunlin: Ma Fu Distributor, 1971), p. 444.
3. Ezekiel 28:12-13, 15-17 NIV.
4. Isaiah 14:12-14 NIV.
5. Revelation 12:7-9 RSV.
6. Hung Pei Chiang, *Ching Wen P'ien Ching Wen* (Taipei: Kung I Publ. Co., 1974), p. 368.
7. Genesis 2:16-17 NIV.
8. Hung Pei Chiang, *Chih Ku Lu Chuan Wen* (Taipei: Lo Tien Publ. Co., 1974), vol. ii, p. 1082.
9. Ma Wei Ching, p. 131.
10. *Ibid.*, p. 1033.
11. Hung Pei Chiang, *Chih Ku Lu Chuan Wen*, vol. ii, p. 959.
12. *Ibid.*, p. 834.
13. *Ibid.*, p. 890.
14. Hung Pei Chiang, *Ching Wen P'ien Ching Wen*, p. 583.
15. Ma Wei Ching, p. 444.
16. Hung Pei Chiang, *Ching Wen P'ien Ching Wen*, p. 551.
17. Hung Pei Chiang, *Chih Ku Lu Chuan Wen*, vol. ii, p. 967.
18. Lin Chih Ch'ing, *Ting Cheng Liu Shu T'ung* (Shanghai: Kuang-I Publ. Co., 1936), section 1, part v, p. 31.
19. *Ibid.*, section 1, part i, p. 14.
20. Genesis 3:1 TEV.
21. Genesis 3:2-3 TEV.
22. Genesis 3:4 NIV.
23. Ma Wei Ching, p. 1357.
24. Genesis 3:5 NIV.
25. Ma Wei Ching, p. 854.
26. *Ibid.*, p. 851.
27. Hung Pei Chiang, *Ching Wen P'ien Ching Wen*, p. 552.

8: The Lethal Bite

1. Genesis 3:6 NKJV.
2. Ma Wei Ching, *Wei Ching Chia Ku Wen Yuan* (Yunlin: Ma Fu Distributor, 1971), p. 134.
3. *Ibid.*, p. 133.
4. *Ibid.*, p. 544.
5. Genesis 3:6 RSV.
6. Hung Pei Chiang, *Ching Wen P'ien Ching Wen* (Taipei: Kung I Publ. Co., 1974), p. 659.
7. Lin Chih Ch'ing, *Ting Cheng Liu Shu T'ung* (Shanghai: Kuang-I Publ. Co., 1936), section 2, part v, p. 2.
8. Ma Wei Chiang, p. 859.
9. Genesis 3:6 RSV.
10. Ma Wei Ching, p. 1033.
11. *Ibid.*, p. 438.
12. Hung Pei Chiang, *Ching Wen P'ien Ching Wen*, p. 340.
13. Genesis 3:7 RSV.
14. Genesis 3:7 TEV.
15. Ma Wei Ching, p. 1055.
16. Lin Chih Ch'ing, section 1, part i, p. 24.
17. *Ibid.*, section 1, part vi, p. 14 under 果 .
18. Genesis 3:8-9 TEV.
19. Hung Pei Chiang, *Ching Wen P'ien Ching Wen,* p. 336.
20. Genesis 3:11 TEV.
21. Ma Wei Ching, p. 659.
22. Hung Pei Ching, p. 661.
23. Genesis 3:12-13 TEV.
24. Genesis 3:15 NKJV.
25. Ma Wei Chiang, *Ching Wen P'ien Ching Wen*, p. 551.
26. Genesis 3:16 NKJV.
27. Ma Wei Ching, p. 130.
28. *Ibid.*
29. Hung Pei Chiang, *Chih Ku Lu Chuan Wen* (Taipei: Lo Tien Publ. Co., 1974), vol. ii. p. 906.
30. Genesis 3:17, 19 NIV.
31. Ma Wei Ching, p. 1232.

32. Hung Pei Chiang, *Ching Wen P'ien Ching Wen*, p. 485.
33. Ma Wei Ching, p. 794.
34. Chung Kuo K'o Hsüeh Yüan K'ao Ku Yen Chiu So Pien Chi, *Chia Ku Wen Pien* (Hong Kong: Chung Hua Shu Chü, 1978), #0783, p. 276.
35. Ma Wei Ching, p. 706
36. Hung Pei Chiang, *Ching Wen P'ien Ching Wen*, p. 215.
38. Ma Wei Ching, p. 737.

9: A Costly Rescue Plan

1. Genesis 3:22-24 NIV.
2. Kung Kuang Lang, *P'ing An We P'u* (Taipei: *Decision Magazine*, December 1985), p. 15.
3. Ma Wei Ching, *Wei Ching Chia Ku Wen Yuan* (Yunlin: Ma Fu Distributor, 1971), p. 1063.
4. Chou Fa Kao, et al., *Ching Wen Ku Lin* (Hong Kong: Chinese University, 1975), p. 6566.
5. Lin Chih Ch'ing, *Ting Cheng Liu Shu T'ung* (Shanghai: Kuang-I Publ. Co., 1936), section 1, part ii, p. 23.
6. Hung Pei Chiang, *Ching Wen P'ien Ching Wen* (Taipei: Kung I Publ. Co., 1974), p. 634.
7. Genesis 3:21 NIV.
8. Ma Wei Ching, p. 1063.
9. *Ibid.*, p. 936.
10. *Ibid.*, p. 1061.
11. *Ibid.*, p. 1060.
12. *Ibid.*, p. 1106.
13. Hung Pei Chiang, *Chih Ku Lu Chuan Wen* (Taipei: Lo Tien Publ. Co., 1974), vol. ii, pp. 1280, 1169.
14. John 1:29 NKJV.
15. Chou Fa Kao, p. 7047.
16. Hung Pei Chiang, *Ching Wen P'ien Ching Wen*, p. 683.
17. Ma Wei Ching, p. 454.
18. *Ibid.*, p. 455.
19. *Ibid.*, p. 889.
20. Lin Chih Ch'ing, section 1, part viii, p. 11.

21. *Ibid.*, part ii, p. 34.
22. Ma Wei Ching, p. 469.
23. Hung Pei Chiang, *Chih Ku Lu Chuan Wen,* vol. ii, p. 1102.
24. *Ibid.*, p. 871.
25. Ma Wei Ching, p. 1231.
26. Lin Chih Ch'ing, section 1, part ii, p. 21.
27. Ma Wei Ching, p. 686.
28. *Ibid.*, p. 683.
29. *Ibid.*, p. 77.
30. Genesis 3:24 NKJV.
31. Exodus 25:22 NKJV.
32. Psalm 80:1 NKJV.
33. Chou Fa Kao, p. 2406.
34. Ma Wei Ching, p. 1023.
35. *Ibid.*, p. 1023.
36. Lin Chih Ch'ing, section 1, part v, p. 10.
37. Ma Wei Ching, p. 1028.
38. *Ibid.*, pp. 1029, 1027.
39. Lin Chih Ch'ing, section 1, part i, p. 23.
40. Leviticus 9:2 RSV.
41. Exodus 29:39 RSV.
42. Genesis 4:2-5 NIV.
43. Ma Wei Ching, p. 504.
44. Genesis 4:15 RSV.
45. Genesis 4:16 NIV.

10: Unraveling a Confucian Puzzle

1. Genesis 3:24 RSV.
2. Ma Wei Ching, *Wei Ching Chia Ku Wen Yuan* (Yunlin: Ma Fu Distributor, 1971), p. 707.
3. Li Hsiao Ting, *Chia Ku Wen Tzu Chi Shih* (Thesis No. 50, Chung Yang Yen Chiu Yuan Li Shih Yan Yu Yan Chiu So, 1965), p. 3235.
4. *Ibid.*, p. 3235.
5. Ma Wei Ching, p. 917.

6. *Ibid.*, p. 919.
7. Chou Fa Kao, et al., *Ching Wen Ku Lin* (Hong Kong: Chinese University, 1975), p. 6568.
8. Lin Chih Ch'ing, *Ting Cheng Liu Shu T'ung* (Shanghai: Kuang-I Publ. Co., 1936), section 1, part ii, p. 30.
9. *Ibid.*, section 1, part v, p. 31.
10. *Ibid.*, section 1, part vii, p. 31 under 介 .
11. *Ibid.*, section 1, part vii, p. 15.
12. Psalm 51:16-17 NIV.
13. James Legge, *The Chinese Classics* (vol. i), *Confucian Analects* (Taipei: Southern Materials Center Inc., 1983), pp. 146, 147.
14. *Ibid.*, p. 206.
15. *Ibid.*, p. 202.
16. *Ibid.*, p. 202.
17. James Legge, *The Chinese Classics* (vol. i), *The Doctrine of the Mean* (Taipei: Southern Materials Center Inc., 1983), p. 404.
18. Lin Chih Ch'ing, section 1, part iii, p. 21.
19. Psalm 104:29-30 NIV.
20. Psalm 146:4 RSV.
21. Daniel 12:2-3 RSV.
22. Isaiah 53 TEV.
23. R. H. Mathews, *Chinese-English Dictionary* (Cambridge, MA: Harvard University Press, thirteenth printing, 1975), p. 1167.

11: The Seed of the Woman

1. Luke 1:30-33 TEV.
2. Luke 1:34 TEV.
3. Luke 1:34-35 TEV.
4. Luke 1:38 TEV.
5. Matthew 1:20-21 TEV.
6. Luke 2:10-12 TEV.
7. Micah 5:2, 4-5 TEV.
8. Matthew 2:8 TEV.

9. Luke 2:46-50 TEV.
10. Luke 2:40 TEV.
11. John 1:29 TEV.
12. 1 Corinthians 11:23-24 TEV.
13. Matthew 26:28-29 TEV.

12: Resolving the Altar of Heaven Mystery

1. Matthew 26:61 TEV.
2. Matthew 26:63-64 NIV.
3. Luke 23:14-16 TEV.
4. Matthew 27:24 TEV.
5. Hebrews 13:12 RSV.
6. Luke 23:34 TEV.
7. Mark 15:34 NIV.
8. John 19:30 NIV.
9. Matthew 27:51-53 TEV.
10. R. H. Mathews, *Chinese-English Dictionary* (Cambridge, MA: Harvard University Press, thirteenth printing, 1975), p. 1167.
11. John 8:12 TEV.
12. John 1:9 NKJV.
13. Hung Pei Chiang, *Chih Ku Lu Chuan Wen* (Taipei: Lo Tien Publ. Co., 1974), vol. ii, p. 1281.
14. *Ibid.*, vol. ii, p. 853.
15. John 3:16 RSV.
16. Matthew 26:26, 28 TEV.
17. John 2:19 NIV.
18. 1 Corinthians 15:22 TEV.
19. Luke 24:50-51 NIV.
20. Acts 1:11 TEV.

13: ShangTi's Last Promise

1. John 14:1-3, 6 TEV.
2. Revelation 21:10-19.
3. Revelation 22:1-2.

4. Revelation 14:1, 3 NKJV.
5. Psalm 99:1-2 NKJV.
6. John 1:1-4, 10-12 TEV.
7. John 10:30 TEV.
8. John 14:8-10 NIV.
9. Ma Wei Ching, *Wei Ching Chia Ku Wen Yuan* (Yunlin: Ma Fu Distributor, 1971), p. 755.
10. *Ibid.*, p. 1044.
11. Matthew 24:3 NKJV.
12. Matthew 24 NKJV.
13. 2 Peter 3:3-4, 7 TEV.
14. Ma Wei Ching, p. 1283.
15. Hung Pei Chiang, *Chih Ku Lu Chuan Wen* (Taipei: Lo Tien Publ. Co., 1974), vol. ii, p. 1032.
16. 1 Thessalonians 4:16-17 TEV.
17. 2 Peter 3:10 TEV.
18. Revelation 21:1-4 TEV.
19. Revelation 22:1-5 TEV.
20. Revelation 22:17 TEV.
21. Revelation 22:14 NKJV.
22. Revelation 2:7 TEV.
23. Romans 8:38-39 TEV.
24. Ma Wei Ching, p. 180.
25. *Ibid.*, p. 183.
26. *Ibid.*, p. 1253.
27. *Ibid.*, p. 180.
28. 1 Peter 2:24 NKJV.
29. Isaiah 45:22-23 TEV.

Epilog

1. Hsu Shen, *Shuo Wen* (Taipei: Li Ming Cultural Enterprises Ltd., 1980), p. 3.
2. *Ibid.*, p. 2.
3. *Ibid.*, p. 105.
4. *Ibid.*, p. 242.
5. *Ibid.*, p. 258.

6. *Ibid.*, p. 272.
7. *Ibid.*, p. 630.
8. *Ibid.*, p. 274.
9. *Ibid.*, p. 595.
10. *Ibid.*, p. 281.
11. *Ibid.*, p. 53.
12. *Ibid.*, p. 639.
13. *Ibid.*, p. 148.
14. *Ibid.*, p. 642.

Appendix

1. Genesis 5:1-11 NKJV.
2. Genesis 6:5-9 NKJV.
3. Genesis 10:25 NKJV.
4. Genesis 11:1, 4-9 NKJV.
5. F. C. Thompson, *A Complete System of Biblical Studies, The New Chain Reference Bible* (Indianapolis: B. B. Kirkbride Bible Co., Inc., 1964), p. 186 (no. 4222-b).
6. R. H. Mathews, *Chinese-English Dictionary* (Cambridge, MA: Harvard University Press, thirteenth printing, 1975), p. 1165.
7. James Legge, *The Chinese Classics* (vol. iii), *The Shoo King: Canon of Shun* (Taipei: Southern Materials Center Inc., 1983), pp. 33, 34.
8. Genesis 10:32 NKJV.

Bibliography

Chou Fa Kao, et al., *Ching Wen Ku Lin*. Hong Kong: Chinese University, 1975.

Chung Kuo K'o Hsüeh Yüan K'ao Ku Yen Chiu So Pien Chi, *Chia Ku Wen Pien*. Hong Kong: Chung Hua Shu Chü, 1978.

Hsin Cheng Yu, *Ancient Chinese History*. Taipei: Taiwan Commercial Press, 1963.

Hsu Shen, *Shuo Wen*. Taipei: Li Ming Cultural Enterprises Ltd., 1980.

Hung Pei Chiang, *Chih Ku Lu Chuan Wen*, vols. I and II. Taipei: Lo Tien Publ. Co., 1974.

Hung Pei Chiang, *Ching Wen P'ien Ching Wen*. Taipei: Kung I Publ. Co., 1974.

Kang, C. H. and Nelson, Ethel R. *The Discovery of Genesis.* Concordia Publishing House, 1979.

Kung Kuang Lang, *P'ing An We P'u.* Taipei: *Decision Magazine*, December 1985.

Legge, James, *The Chinese Classics* (vol. III), *The Shoo King: Canon of Shun.* Taipei: Southern Materials Center Inc., 1983.

Legge, James, *The Chinese Classics* (vol. I), *The Doctrine of the Mean.* Taipei: Southern Materials Center Inc., 1983.

Legge, James, *The Chinese Classics* (vol. I), *Confucian Analects.* Taipei: Southern Materials Center Inc., 1983.

Legge, James, *The Notions of the Chinese Concerning God and Spirits.* Hong Kong: Hong Kong Register Office, 1852.

Li Hsiao Ting, *Chia Ku Wen Tzu Chi Shih.* Thesis No. 50, Chung Yang Yen Chiu Yuan Li Shih Yan Yu Yan Chiu So, 1965.

Lin Chih Ch'ing, *Ting Cheng Liu Shu T'ung.* Shanghai: Kuang-I Publ. Co., 1936.

Lung Ch'uan Kwei T'ai Lang, *Shih Chi Hui Chu K'ao Cheng.* Taipei: Han Ching Wen Hua Enterprise Co. Ltd., 1983.

Mathews, R. H., *Chinese-English Dictionary.* Cambridge, MA: Harvard University Press, thirteenth printing, 1975.

Ma Wei Ching, *Wei Ching Chia Ku Wen Yuan.* Yunlin: Ma Fu Distributor, 1971.

Smith, Bradley and Weng, Wan-go, *China, a History in Art.* New York: Doubleday, 1972.

Thompson, Frank C., *A Complete System of Biblical Studies, The New Chain Reference Bible.* Indianapolis: B. B. Kirkbride Bible Co., 1964.

Wilder, G. D., and Ingram, J. H., *Analysis of Chinese Characters.* Taipei: Chin Wen Publ. Co., 1964.

Character Summary

Pagination cited is for the first appearance of each character in the text. All characters follow dictionary English definitions except for an occasional definition, placed in quotes, assigned by the authors.

Character	English Equivalent	Page
上帝 卐 卂卐	ShangTi, God, Heavenly Ruler	13, 30, 130, 131
帝 卐 卂卐	Emperor	16, 30, 130, 131
上	above	16
¥	produce, bring forth, create	29
Ψ	"God"	19, 34, 37, 44
♦ ◇ △ ⊥ ◯	ground, dust, earth	29, 32-33
⊔ ▽ ◯ ▢ ◇ ▽	mouth, person	30
¥	speak, tell	29
示申 示 示 示	Shen, God	31, 44-45, 65
示 示 丁 示	God radical	31, 45, 48
⺕ ⺊ ∈ ∋ ⺕ ⺕ ∋ ∈ ∃	hand(s)	31-32, 42, 60 82, 56, 85

	instruct	31, 45, 65
•	adult male	31
	hole, pit	32
	great, noble man	32, 35
	create, start, found, immediately	32
	moment, instant	32
	great	32
	body	33
	person, being	32-33, 41, 43, 70-71
⊙	sun, person	33
☉	dawn, early morning	33
	fire	34, 36, 47, 55, 86
	to be like	34
	T'ien, heaven	35
	naked, red	36
	intelligent, civilized	36
	father	36, 45, 50 54, 56
	father, garden, beginning	37, 77
	vessel	37, 41
≡	breath	38
	breath	38
	cause, excellent	38-39
	"man"	39

secret, private, alone	53, 74
negative, no, not	72
magnanimous, expansive	72
dread, fear	72
beautiful	73
fruit, consequence, result, effect	73
desire, covet	73
beginning	74
weak, yielding	74
might as well	75
disobedient	75
avail oneself of	75
clothes	75-76
naked	76
fruit	76
come	76
stumble, fall	76
ashamed	77
seed, offspring	77
sorrow	78
piece	78
difficult, trouble, worry	79
mourn	79
death	79
in consequence of, because	79
face-to-face	80
"mount"	79-80